# THE ESSENCE OF JUDAISM

# THE ESSENCE OF JUDAISM

BY

I. E. KING

'By three distinctive signs we trace the members of the Jewish race, a tender heart, self-reverence, and practical benevolence'—(*Yebomoth*, 79*a*).

LONDON
THE SONCINO PRESS
FIVE GOWER STREET
1935

PRINTED IN ENGLAND BY
HENDERSON AND SPALDING LTD
LONDON SE 15

THIS BOOK IS DEDICATED IN EVER-LOVING DEVOTION TO MY DEAR MOTHER, AND TO THE SACRED MEMORY OF MY DEAR FATHER (HYMAN KING ז״ל) AND UNCLE (HARRIS KING ז״ל), WHOSE EXEMPLARY CONDUCT OF LIFE HAS INSTILLED INTO ME A LOVE FOR GOD, MY RELIGION, AND MY NEIGHBOUR

# CONTENTS

# PREFACE

During the years in which I have been occupied in teaching, both privately and at the classes of the Higher Crumpsall Synagogue, Manchester, I have very often been requested to recommend a book suitable for private study which deals with the doctrines and observances of Judaism. Of the books procurable some are far too elaborate, whilst others, although well adapted for providing a general knowledge of Judaism, are lacking in detail. At an Educational Conference which was held in Manchester other teachers stated that they were also suffering from the lack of suitable religious books which they could use in their classrooms, or put into the hands of their pupils for private study.

My purpose, therefore, in writing this book was to supply this much-felt need, and also to provide those of my co-religionists, who are for any reason unable to study the larger works, with a book which will clearly explain to them the meaning of the doctrines and observances of Judaism, and will arouse in them feelings of love and respect towards our ancient faith.

Having inherited, from my late father ז״ל, a heartfelt love for God and His Torah, I rejoice in having this opportunity of magnifying His name, and proclaiming the greatness of the Torah, that wonderful treasure which was granted by God to us, His chosen nation. May it be His will to grant His blessing to my humble effort to instil into the hearts of my readers an understanding of His abounding mercy and loving kindness, and a realisation of the tremendous debt of love and gratitude which we owe to Him, our Heavenly Father, for the continual guardianship and support which He bestows upon us.

The lessons from the Rabbis have been carefully chosen for the valuable moral lessons which they convey.

The late Rabbi S. R. Hirsch, when dealing in his book *Nineteen Letters of Ben Uziel* with the growing indifference to Judaism, wrote: ' There is one way to salvation, where the sin was committed the atonement must begin and this one way is, to forget the inherited prejudices and opinions concerning Judaism; to go back to the sources of Judaism, to Bible, Talmud and Midrash; to read, study and comprehend them in order to live them; to draw from them the teachings of Judaism concerning God, the world, mankind and Israel, according to history and precept; to know Judaism out of itself; to learn from its own utterances its science of life.' It is my earnest hope that the contents of this book will prove of assistance to those who are desirous of acting upon the advice of this eminent teacher in Israel. If my humble effort will, to some extent, check the present-day drift away from religion, then I shall have been amply repaid for my labour.

I take this opportunity of acknowledging my grateful thanks to Mr. H. M. Adler, M.A., LL.M., for the valuable time spent in reading my MS., and to Rev. Dr. A. Cohen, M.A., Rabbi Dr. I. Epstein, B.A., Rabbi Dr. S. M. Lehrman, M.A., Rabbi I. Abrahams, M.A., and the Rev. J. Pereira-Mendoza, B.A., for the praise and encouragement which they have given me in connection with my work.

I. E. KING.

Manchester, 8.

## CHAPTER I

# THE HONOUR OF BEING A JEW

IT IS an honour to be a member of the Jewish Nation because it was the Jews who were chosen by God as His Special People, at a time when all other peoples were idol-worshippers and religiously ignorant. The Jews were deemed worthy of receiving that wonderful treasure, the Torah (תּוֹרָה), from which men derive the great blessings of righteousness, freedom and friendship towards one another. The religion of the Jew is based on the teachings of the Torah ; and we, as members of the Jewish people, accordingly live a religion of life; a religion of glory; a religion of mercy not only to human beings but even towards animals. We were appointed by God as His messengers or missionaries, and it therefore became our duty to teach the peoples the supremacy of God, and the lessons contained in the Torah. Powerful nations like the Egyptians, Babylonians, Romans and others, have done their utmost to destroy us and make us forsake our God, but their efforts were in vain, and the Jew and his Torah continue to exist although their oppressors have long since perished.

We should indeed feel honoured when we realise that, notwithstanding the agonies which we have been forced to bear, we have persevered in our task as Missionaries of God, have convinced almost all civilised nations of the folly of worshipping or believing in idols, and have spread a knowledge of the Ten Commandments and the divine qualities of mercy, justice and truth. These commandments and qualities have been embodied in the laws of civilised nations, and we can therefore claim that the spiritual knowledge which we, the Jewish people, have spread has enlightened the darkness of the nations, and has led them to forsake idols and place their faith in the Living Everlasting God.

It is most important, however, that we should continually remember that our selection as God's chosen people is dependent upon our fulfilment of the laws and commandments of the Torah. If we prove ourselves to be obedient followers of its teachings, then we shall continue to remain a selected nation and be worthy of God's special favour; but if we neglect its teachings, then our selection will cease and we shall become objects of God's disfavour. We should therefore zealously guard the honour which has been bestowed upon us, by observing our religion and keeping its Sabbaths and Festivals; by guarding both our words and actions from bringing shame or dishonour upon the name of our nation; by obeying the Torah, that gift from God which has meant, and does still mean, so very much to us; and by causing the Almighty God to be recognised as the Supreme Power, Protector and Saviour of all humanity.

## CHAPTER II

# THE TEN COMMANDMENTS

YOU HAVE most certainly read, or heard, how God led the Israelites, or Jewish people, in their wanderings through the wilderness; and how He brought them to Mount Sinai. There, with great wonders, He gave them, through Moses, their earthly leader, the two tables of stone upon which were written the Ten words, or Commandments (עֲשֶׂרֶת הַדִּבְּרוֹת). In the following chapters we shall read what those commandments were, and the lessons which they should teach us.

### THE FIRST COMMANDMENT

*I am the Lord thy God, who brought thee out of the land of Egypt, out of the house of bondage.*

The God who gave this commandment had released the Israelites from the Egyptian slavery, but He was also the creator of the world and all it contained. Why, therefore, did He only introduce Himself as the God who had delivered them?

It was necessary for Him to introduce Himself in this manner, because He had a very important message to deliver which would best be emphasised by such an introduction. The Israelites had lived in Egypt for hundreds of years, and the Egyptians had possessed idols and certain animals which they worshipped as gods; and which they asserted were the creators of the world and all it contained. They prayed to them whenever they were in need of assistance, and firmly believed that it was they who granted them the fulfilment of their desires. If, therefore, God had introduced Himself as the creator of all things, then the Israelites would have thought Him to be one of the Egyptian gods. By being told, however, that He was the God who had delivered them from the Egyptian slavery, they understood that He was far greater and mightier than the greatest or mightiest god of the Egyptians. They were also reminded by this introduction of all that He had done for their sakes; by helping them to cross the Red Sea, bringing water from a rock, and providing them from heaven with manna.

This commandment should convey a greater message to us than it did to our forefathers. They had suffered as slaves in Egypt only for hundreds of years; whilst we, the Jewish nation, have been forced to suffer even worse than slaves for thousands of years, as the result of the cruel passions of many nations. We have twice been deprived of our land; our temples have been destroyed, and we have been scattered amongst all the nations of the world. We have been forced to suffer at the hands of the Babylonians, Syrians, and

Romans; the Crusaders massacred us and the Spaniards tortured and burned us; and now the German nation has also turned against us. We have been tortured and oppressed in every generation, and nations have shown their hatred against us by heaping disgrace upon us and punishing us for remaining true to our God and His Torah. Yet in spite of all efforts to destroy us, we are still in existence, because of the guardianship of God who has delivered us from their evil powers and intentions.

This commandment, therefore, should remind us that the Almighty Merciful God has not only helped our forefathers to live through the years of Egyptian slavery and, after delivering them with great miracles and wonders, fulfilled His promise to Abraham to lead them to Canaan, but also, that He has helped *us* to live through the generations of oppression which *we* have been made to suffer, and that He has promised, when the time will be pleasing before Him, to deliver *us* with great wonders from the long and painful exile which we have been forced to bear by leading *us* back to the land of Canaan, which is now called Palestine.

Have you noticed that God used the word 'thee' instead of the word 'you'? If He had used the word 'you', then each person could have said that as in Hebrew grammar the word 'you' is used when addressing more than one person, God had not meant *him* to obey the commandments, and would have tried to find excuses. God, therefore, purposely used the word ' thee ', which clearly points out that each person is in duty bound to obey them.

The thoughts, which this commandment causes to arise in our minds, should teach us to put our whole faith in God as our continual guardian and helper. We should remember that He has answered the prayers of those who trusted in Him and prayed to Him with all their hearts and minds, and we shall then be encouraged to address heartfelt prayers to Him at all times, and firmly to believe that He is the only One to whom we should pray and in whom we should put our complete trust.

## The Second Commandment

*Thou shalt have no other gods before me. Thou shalt not make unto thee a graven image; nor the form of anything that is in the heaven above, or that is in the earth beneath, or that is in the water under the earth; thou shalt not bow down thyself unto them, nor serve them; for I the Lord thy God am a jealous God, visiting the iniquity of the fathers upon the children upon the third and upon the fourth generation, unto them that hate me: and showing loving-kindness to the thousandth generation, unto them that love me and keep my commandments.*

At the time when this commandment was given to the Israelites they had been away from Egypt only a very short period. There, as you have already read, idols and certain animals were worshipped as gods, and it was necessary, therefore, to warn the Israelites against imitating what they had seen done in Egypt. An idol is a figure of a human being, animal or fish, which is deemed worthy of being worshipped or venerated.

Although this commandment was given to our forefathers thousands of years ago, it has been disobeyed in every generation and even we have persons amongst us who are idol worshippers. Many persons are possessed by an unlimited desire to accumulate money, and are prepared even to desecrate the Sabbath and Festivals to satisfy this desire. They refuse to contribute towards charitable needs and are entirely obsessed by the craving for monetary gain; others do not hesitate to disobey the commandments of God because they interfere with their pleasure or convenience. In this way money, pleasure and convenience, being of such supreme importance that even the will of God is disregarded for their sakes, can be called idols, and those who love them so fervently can be called idol-worshippers.

This commandment teaches us that we are forbidden to regard any person, animal, or thing as being worthy of our worship. We must cast away from our minds the thought that there exists another power which is equal or superior to the power of God, and we must carefully guard our speech from even seeming to insinuate that we doubt His Unity. Every thought which we permit to strengthen in our minds, in fear of the power of any person, causes us to lessen our belief and trust in the supreme power of the Almighty God; since, if we truly trusted in Him, we should not have permitted such thoughts to trouble us. As all persons are merely human, and therefore unable to do or know that which is beyond human powers, we are not permitted to attach any importance to fortune-tellers, or any persons who claim magic powers.

We are warned that God visits the iniquities of the fathers upon the children. These words must not be understood as they are written, but must be regarded as containing a great moral lesson. The Merciful God, whose care and kindness is everlasting and bestowed upon everyone, would not punish one person for the sins committed by another. What these words really tell us is that He will watch the children of those who sin against Him, and will notice their efforts to improve upon the behaviour of their parents. That God is not eager to punish those who sin we are taught by the words ‘ upon the third and upon the fourth generation ’, which teach us that He will mercifully withhold punishment even until the fourth generation, in the hope that they will turn from their evil ways, and again make Him the object of their gratitude and devotion by obeying His will. That He does not punish a child for the sins of his parents is proved by the words: ‘The soul that sinneth, it shall die: the son shall not bear the iniquity of the father, neither shall the father bear the iniquity of the son; the righteousness of the righteous shall be upon him. But if the wicked turn from all his sins that he hath committed, and keep all my statutes and do that which is lawful and right, he shall surely live, he shall not die' (Ezekiel, xviii, 20, 21). In these words are indicated His abounding mercy to all, and His promise of forgiveness to those who sincerely repent of their sins and practise good deeds.

We are also warned that He is a jealous God, but as jealousy is a great sin and a quality not to be admired, we must seek a deeper meaning in these words also. God had brought the Israelites from slavery to freedom and attended to all their needs, and He therefore resented their worshipping idols, and showing to them the gratitude and devotion which were due to Him. We should therefore understand the words 'I, the Lord thy God, am a jealous God', as meaning that He would not permit the love and devotion which was due to Him to be shared by or given to any idol.

## CHAPTER III

# THE TEN COMMANDMENTS (*continued*)

### The Third Commandment

*Thou shalt not take the name of the Lord thy God in vain; for the Lord will not hold him guiltless that taketh His name in vain.*

This commandment forbids us to mention the name of God unless it is absolutely essential for us to do so. We are forbidden to utter such expressions as 'Oh God!' or 'Good God!', etc., etc. On those occasions when we are permitted to mention His name, such as during our prayers or for other sacred purposes, we must do so with the utmost reverence and respect, as otherwise we become guilty of taking the name of God in vain. We are forbidden to swear at all, unless it is in a Court of Justice. Matters of very great importance are often decided by a judge, and we are called upon to tell all that we know concerning the matter, and have to swear by the holy name of God that we will tell the truth. On such occasions we must take the utmost care that we tell exactly what we saw, heard or know; and all our words should be uttered only after the greatest consideration. If we deny the truth, or wilfully utter misleading statements, then we become guilty of grievously sinning against God, by whose name we have sworn to speak truthfully. We are not permitted to swear that a stone is a stone, or other such obvious oaths, as in this way we take the name of God in vain.

We should continually do our very utmost to glorify the name of God, by causing our actions to shed honour upon it. We have been chosen by God as His special people, and it is therefore our duty to set examples to those with whom we come in contact. If we do our utmost to fulfil the teachings of our religion, and prove through our actions that we are possessed of the qualities of goodness, kindness and honesty, then we not only shed honour and glory upon ourselves, but also upon the great name of God. This is termed in Hebrew קִדּוּשׁ הַשֵּׁם, 'Sanctification of God's name'.

## The Fourth Commandment

*Remember the Sabbath day to keep it holy. Six days shalt thou labour, and do all thy work: but the seventh day is a Sabbath unto the Lord thy God: in it thou shalt not do any work, thou, nor thy son, nor thy daughter, thy manservant, nor thy maidservant, nor thy cattle, nor the stranger that is within thy gates: for in six days the Lord made heaven and earth, the sea and all that is therein, and rested on the seventh day: wherefore the Lord blessed the Sabbath day and hallowed it.*

This commandment teaches us that we must spend the Sabbath day in rest and holiness, and that we should endeavour on it to become spiritually refreshed by means of religious study. Observe here the kindness and mercy of our Heavenly Father, who provides all creatures with their needs, and has especially commanded us concerning those who are less fortunate than ourselves, by distinctly mentioning the servant and animal as equals with us in the duty of resting on this holy day.

By the words ' Six days shalt thou labour ', we are taught the dignity of work and that it is sinful before God wilfully to idle our days and neglect the opportunities afforded us by Him of making full use of the time which He grants us. It is only after working during the six days that we are able really to enjoy the wonderful gift of a day of rest, as a result of which we shall prove more fit and prepared to resume our work. The merciful God knew this, and He therefore commanded us to work for six days and rest on the seventh, and in this way we enjoy both our work and our rest.

We are only permitted to work on the Sabbath day, or desecrate its holiness, if a life is at stake, but not for any other reason than a matter of life and death. This is best explained by an incident in the life of Rabbi Hillel. During the time that he was yet a student he supported himself by working as a woodcutter. The small amount of money which he earned was divided between supporting himself and paying the admission fee to the doorkeeper of the House of

Study. One Friday he had not earned sufficient for his needs, and was therefore unable to gain admission to hear the lecture which was being given. He therefore climbed up to a window of the lecture-room and became so engrossed in what he heard that he remained there entirely unaware of a heavy fall of snow. When the Rabbis arrived on the following day to deliver their lectures they were greatly surprised to find the room darker than usual, until they observed the figure of a man pressed against the window. When he was brought down he was found to be frozen with cold. The Rabbis immediately prepared a fire and a hot bath, with the help of which they soon brought him back to consciousness.

## The Fifth Commandment

*Honour thy father and thy mother: that thy days may be long upon the land which the Lord thy God giveth thee.*

This commandment teaches us that it is our duty to love and honour our parents, and willingly obey their wishes. There are no other persons who can claim the love and respect which is their due, as from the hour of our birth they care for us and provide our every need; they suffer pain and anxiety for our sakes, and are ever ready even to endanger their health in order to protect us from illness. We should not wait, therefore, to be commanded to show them due regard, as our own sense of thankfulness towards them should not permit us to do otherwise. We must not speak disrespectfully to them or utter words of disrespect about them, but we must value their opinions and advice and do our utmost to make our actions pleasing to them.

We are only obliged to disobey our parents when they desire us to perform that which is contrary to the will of God, as the desires of God demand even greater respect and obedience than the desires of our parents. On such an occasion we should do all in our power to convince them that we are not disobeying them because we lack respect for them, but because their desires are in conflict with the desires of God, our Heavenly Father, to whose will we owe even greater respect than we do to theirs.

During our childhood, when we are weak and helpless, or even later, when we have become stronger but are still unable to provide ourselves with all our needs, it is our parents who guard us and provide us with our necessities and comforts. It is therefore our duty, when we are capable of being of some assistance to them, to do our utmost willingly to repay them for their kindnesses and sacrifices on our behalf. When they have become advanced in years and weak, or are unable to provide for themselves, we must guard them from all dangers and worries, and provide them with food, clothes, and every comfort. If we are financially unable to provide them with necessities, or if they do not require our help, then we should not make this an excuse for neglecting them altogether, as we are still able to honour and cherish them and shower our heartfelt love upon them.

The duty of honouring our parents continues even after they have departed from this world. After death the souls, which are the sparks of God which He had put into their bodies so that they should live and be capable of thinking, feeling, reasoning, and directing their every action and emotion, return to the loving care of their Creator; there to receive their recompense for the manner in which they used the precious gift of life which He had granted to them. If, therefore, we do our best to fulfil the commandments of God; offer charity and consolation to the distressed, and do other good deeds; then their souls are rewarded, and people honour their memory; because it is chiefly as a result of their teachings that we have learnt our duty to God, and the kindness which we should show to our fellow beings.

The respect which has to be shown to parents should also, to some extent, be shown to our guardians, teachers, or other such people who stand to us in their places. We must particularly show our respect to our religious teachers who make us acquainted with the moral and spiritual lessons of our religion; we should grant them our whole attention, trying to fulfil what they teach us, and appreciating the trouble they take to inculcate into us those duties which we are called upon to perform as members of the Jewish nation.

To honour and obey our parents is, besides being a pleasant and natural duty, also of great advantage to us, as we are promised that God will reward us with long life. It is also related that when the Israelites entered the land of Canaan all the twelve tribes assembled on Mount Ebal, and the Priests and Levites cursed the child who neglected to honour its parents, and all the Israelites answered 'Amen', which means 'so be it'. We should observe this duty, however, out of the heartfelt love and respect we possess for them, and not because of the reward which we have been promised for doing so.

## CHAPTER IV

# THE TEN COMMANDMENTS (*continued*)

### The Sixth Commandment

*Thou shalt not murder.*

This commandment not only forbids us to take the life of any person, but even to plot his death in any way. Life is a most valuable gift from God, and we must not destroy it even by taking our own life, but we must endeavour to make the best use of it until the time comes when He will reclaim it from us. The prohibition of causing an injury is also included in this commandment, as it will perhaps cause the death of the person, and we will then become guilty of murder. When a person is angry with another he will perhaps, in order to obtain revenge for a past offence, pick a quarrel with him and attack him, and in the course of the fight he may, in the heat of his passion, strike the other person a blow which will either kill him instantly or cause his death at a later date. Such feelings of anger, hatred, or revenge are therefore most certainly forbidden, and must be uprooted from our hearts and minds.

We must continually guard ourselves when speaking against uttering any words which may put a person to shame in the presence of others; as even if the words were not so intended, they very often lead to serious results. It may happen, for instance, that during a party, when all present are enjoying themselves, a friend in play hides something which is your property, and, understanding that no harm is intended, you exclaim in a jovial manner, ' Bring that back, you thief '; both of you realising, of course, that the word ' thief ' is not to be taken seriously. Later, perhaps, your friend will attend another party where something will really be stolen, and someone will exclaim: ' He (your friend) must have taken it, as I have heard him called a thief ', being under the impression that you had really meant what your words implied, and so, because of them, your friend is now in a most unenviable position and is publicly put to shame. Any action or word which causes the disgrace of a person before other people makes us guilty of what is termed in Hebrew (שְׁפִיכוּת דָּמִים) ' The shedding of blood '.

We must be ever ready to assist those who are in need either of money or food, and must offer consolation to those who are mentally distressed. By performing our duty to the needy we sometimes save their lives, whilst our neglect would perhaps have caused them to die of hunger, or to take their own lives in order to escape from their misery, and in such a case we would be responsible for their death. We must take great care to avoid taking part in, or advising, an act which can lead to the ruin of another person. How much more peace and happiness there would be in the world if every person continually kept in mind the lessons of this commandment and did his utmost to obey them. War, in which one nation seeks to kill and injure another nation, would cease for ever; and all people would live in peace and friendship with their neighbours. May God cause everyone to understand the greatness and wisdom of His Commandments, and fill their hearts with love and devotion towards Him, and a desire for the welfare of their neighbours.

## The Seventh Commandment

*Thou shalt not commit adultery.*

This commandment teaches us that husbands and wives must be faithful to one another, and find pleasure in the company of each other. It also teaches us that we are not permitted to read books which are immoral, or excite in us thoughts which are not pure; and that our friends must be chosen from amongst those who are of good and decent life. You will perhaps think that the kind of books which you read is of no great consequence, or that there is no necessity to pick and choose amongst your friends, as you will perhaps regard yourself as able to withstand the power of evil examples. But experience has taught that wicked or indecent friends cause us to become so accustomed to seeing sinful actions being committed, that we find ourselves habitually following their example. Our language, both during private or public conversation, should be decent and proper; and only pure words and expressions should be uttered by us. Our conduct and general behaviour should always be honourable, and serve as examples to all with whom we come in contact. We should do our utmost to keep the precious gift of purity which God has granted to each one of us, and not to be persuaded to part with it by the mockery of the scorners. Once it has been lost, it can rarely, if ever, be regained.

## The Eighth Commandment

*Thou shalt not steal.*

This commandment teaches us that we are forbidden to take anything which is the property of another person, unless we have obtained the permission of its owner to do so. We must guard ourselves against stealing our neighbours' thoughts by pretending to be kind and sympathetic towards him in order to become acquainted with his private affairs; or by seeking to gain information with the intention of using it against the informant. We should also avoid causing our neighbour to have a false impression, even if we do not harm him thereby. A Rabbi was one day walking with his disciples, and met, at some distance from the town, a very learned man. This man thought that as the Rabbi was walking in the direction of his house, he must have intended honouring him with a visit, and so he thanked the Rabbi for his intended honour. ‘ Do not thank me,’ replied the Rabbi, ‘ as my purpose was merely to enjoy the walk and not to visit you.’ The man felt greatly humiliated, and the disciples therefore asked the Rabbi why he had caused the man to be put to shame before them. ‘ Would it not have been better ’, they asked, ‘ if you had permitted him to continue to think you had intended to visit him ? ’ ‘ Would you have me guilty of telling an untruth ? ’ said the Rabbi. ‘ Certainly not,’ they replied, ‘ but you could have remained silent.’ ‘ My children,’ replied the Rabbi, ‘ it is very wrong to accept a reward which is not our due; or to create either by our words or silence a false thought in the mind of any person.’

We are forbidden to steal persons and sell them into slavery. Until the nations united against this cruel traffic in human beings, the market-places were filled with them and they were publicly sold into slavery. These slaves were very often thrashed without mercy, and sometimes even to death, by the cruel people whom they were forced to serve. In some parts of the world people are still being bought and sold into slavery, and this is a great cause of misery to thousands of human beings.

When some shopkeepers observe that customers are anxious to purchase certain articles, they charge more for them than they originally intended; others cheat their customers by giving them short weight, or by supplying a faulty article in the place of a perfect one which has already been purchased. These actions are strictly forbidden, and would cause them to be as guilty of stealing as if they had stolen the purse or some other article belonging to the customer. People are often engaged to do some work and are paid at an hourly rate; such people are forbidden to waste time in order to increase their earnings. Although we may think that our sins will remain undetected or unobserved, and that we shall therefore escape punishment, we must remember that God knows and sees our every action, and that He is continually aware of the efforts which we make to live good and honourable lives.

## CHAPTER V

# THE TEN COMMANDMENTS (*continued*)

### The Ninth Commandment

*Thou shalt not bear false witness against thy neighbour.*

This commandment forbids us to speak falsely against our neighbour. We must strictly avoid the repeating of evil reports as it sometimes happens that a person, either through jealousy or for his own advantage, will invent an evil report against another person, and by repeating it we shall thereby be helping him in his evil intention.

Sometimes when questioned regarding the truth of a report, instead of stating openly that it is false, we merely smile, in the hope that the enquirer will think it is true, and will at the same time think well of us for not desiring to speak evil of anyone. Such actions are to be despised and are included as forbidden in this commandment.

The telling of an untruth, even if not meant to harm anyone, is also forbidden, as it is liable to injure a person unintentionally. A liar is far more to be feared than a thief, as the property which has been stolen can in most cases be recovered, whilst the damage caused by an untrue statement can rarely, if ever, be rectified. The untruth will have been passed on from one person to another, and it will therefore prove an impossibility to correct the damage which has been done.

An untrue or false person is not even trusted or liked by the people whom his falsehood has benefited. They are aware of his disregard for the truth and therefore fear to associate with him, lest he will commence to scatter false reports about them, as he has done about other people. We should therefore do our best continually to bear in mind the teachings of this commandment, as they will prove of the greatest advantage both to us and to our neighbour. We should repeat with all our hearts the words 'O my God ! guard my tongue from evil and my lips from speaking deceitfully'.

## The Tenth Commandment

*Thou shalt not covet thy neighbour's house, thou shalt not covet thy neighbour's wife, nor his manservant, nor his maidservant, nor his ox, nor his ass, nor anything that is thy neighbour's.*

This commandment forbids us to desire the property of another person. If that person is richer than we are, or has a nicer home or more possessions than we possess, then we must realise that those possessions are his through the blessing of God, and most probably through hard work. We are not forbidden, however, to be ambitious, or to nourish the desire of bettering ourselves; but we must pray for the blessing of the Almighty Merciful God, the Giver of all things, and that He should grant success to our honest efforts to obtain those possessions which will prove to our advantage.

It is very wrong of us to desire a thing which is the property of another person. If our neighbour possesses a beautiful house, and we say 'We would like a similar house to this one', then we have not sinned, as there are many other houses of a similar kind which we can purchase; but if we say 'We like this house and would be pleased if it was ours', then we have indeed sinned, as we are particularly desirous of obtaining our neighbour's property.

The desire to obtain that which is the property of another person is very often the cause of robbery, murder, and many other crimes. The Bible contains an excellent example of the danger of covetousness. A king called Ahab desired a vineyard which belonged to one of his subjects, but the man refused either to sell or give it to the king. Jezebel, the wife of Ahab, therefore arranged a plot in which false evidence was to be given against the owner of the vineyard (this is forbidden in the ninth commandment), and as a result of this evidence he was stoned to death and Ahab obtained the vineyard which he so greatly desired. God was very angry with them for their evil actions, and severely punished them.

We must always thank God for the life and health which He grants us as these are undoubtedly the most precious possessions. We should feel satisfied and happy with all we already possess, and trust that when we have done all in our power to help ourselves God will also bestow His blessing on our efforts.

## CHAPTER VI

# THE SHEMA (שְׁמַע)

THE Shema, which is one of the most important of our prayers, is made up of three portions, all of which are taken from the Torah, or Five Books of Moses (Deuteronomy, vi, 4-9; xi, 13-21; Numbers, xv, 37-41). It is recited during our morning and evening prayers, and before retiring at night; and it is a custom to cover the eyes whilst saying the first line: 'Hear, O Israel, the Lord our God, the Lord is One'. This is done in order that our minds should be entirely concentrated upon the meaning of what is being said; and also to emphasise that, notwithstanding the lack of visible proof, we are firmly convinced of the Unity of God. The Shema also teaches us that we should love our God with all our hearts, souls and might; that we should teach His laws and commandments; and that we shall be rewarded if we obey His will or punished if we disobey Him. We should not, however, merely love our Merciful Heavenly Father because we have been commanded to do so, but we should bear in mind the deliverances and wonders which He has performed for our forefathers and the daily life, care and support which He so graciously grants us, and we shall then be filled with heartfelt love and gratitude towards Him. To love God with all our souls has been explained by our Rabbis as meaning that we are in duty bound to love Him even at the cost of our lives. We should be ever ready to follow the examples set us by those Jewish martyrs who suffered great tortures and even death for the love of God and His Torah. They were promised great riches and honours if they would consent to forsake Him and neglect His commandments, while the severest tortures or death by burning would otherwise be their fate; they could not, however, be moved, and with the Unity of God upon their lips they proved ready to sacrifice their lives for His holy name.

The Emperor Hadrian issued a decree forbidding the study of the Torah on pain of death, but Rabbi Akiba possessed too great a love for this study to be deterred by this decree. As a punishment he was condemned to death by torture, but although in terrible agony, he heroically repeated the words of the Shema and explained to his disciples that he was delighted to be able to prove his sincere love for God by readily forfeiting even his life for His sake. We who live in a land of religious freedom do not suffer such decrees, and are not called upon to undergo such sacrifices for the sake of our religious convictions, but we are capable of showing our willingness to suffer, if need be, for our God by sacrificing those desires and pleasures which would lead us to forsake Him or His commandments.

The words, 'And thou shalt speak of them when thou sittest in thine house, and when thou walkest by the way, and when thou liest down, and when thou risest up', should teach us that it is not sufficient for us only to think of the words and commands of God when we are standing in prayer or at other fixed times, but that it is our duty to remember them at all times and in all places. We must permit them to guide us in all our actions, and to influence our every thought.

The desire for reward, or that we should be honoured and well thought of by other people, should not be the motive of our obedience to the will of God, as such behaviour is hateful before Him. Feelings of obedience must be aroused in us because we possess a heartfelt love towards Him, which does not permit us to disobey His will or incur His anger.

These teachings should be borne in mind by us when we are reading the Shema, and should be fulfilled by us as loving children of our Merciful Father. In a future chapter we shall read of three important duties which are also commanded in this prayer.

## CHAPTER VII

# CHARITY

THE teachings of our religion impress upon us that all men are really brethren, as we have One Father, and He created us all; we should therefore regard it as our duty to assist all who are in need and to do our utmost to ease their sufferings. During the time that our forefathers lived in Palestine they were commanded to leave the gleanings, and the produce of the corners of their fields, in order that the needy should benefit by gathering it. They were also commanded to put aside for the needy a tenth of their increase at the end of every three years, and to grant them many other benefits.

We have been deprived of our land, and are unable to bestow on the needy any benefits from fields or harvests; in order therefore to fulfil our duty to those unfortunate people we must grant them a share of our profits, and help to supply them with food, clothing and other necessities. We should not wait until they come to beg for our assistance, but we should ourselves search them out. Many persons are ashamed to appeal for assistance, as they do not wish their distress to become known to others, and unless we search them out they will perhaps die of want. To such persons it is far better to lend money than to offer charity, as in this way they will be led to suppose that you are unaware how great is the need in which they find themselves and will thus be saved from shame. They will accept the money which you offer to lend them, and will satisfy their needs, and will then put their trust in God to enable them to repay you. By performing such an action you will have done three excellent deeds; you will have eased their distress, saved them from shame, and caused them to again put their heartfelt trust in the loving care and great power of God. We are strictly forbidden to claim or accept interest on money which has been lent by us to a needy person.

Our charity should be given, if possible, in such a manner that the receiver will not know who has assisted him, as he will then be spared the shame which he would otherwise feel when he met his benefactor. This manner of charity was adopted by many of our Rabbis. One Rabbi placed money on the doorsteps of the poor, whilst another Rabbi carried a cloth over his shoulder which contained a number of knots in which money had been enclosed; the poor were thus enabled to obtain assistance by undoing the knots and taking the money, whilst the Rabbi did not know whom he had assisted.

Our gifts to the poor should always be accompanied by cheerful and sympathetic looks, as shame and distress are likely to be felt by the receiver if the gift is made with a sour expression.

God has promised to reward the giving of charity, as we are told: 'Thou shalt surely give him (the needy person) and thine heart shall not be grieved when thou givest unto him, because that for this thing the Eternal, thy God, shall bless thee in all thy works, and in every performance of thy hand' (Deuteronomy, xv, 10).

There are many persons who are sad or downhearted because of some trouble which has befallen them; to such persons it is our duty to speak words of comfort and encouragement. We should explain to them the great kindness and mercy of our Heavenly Father, and that He would not have permitted the trouble to occur unless He had a definite purpose in so doing; we should urge them to put their heartfelt trust in Him, and remind them of the words: 'The Lord is nigh to all those who call upon Him, *to all who call upon Him in truth*' (Psalm cxlv, 18).

When a person is ill we should visit him, and, after speaking words of good cheer, we should do our best to help him to realise that God is a great and powerful healer, and that he should pray to Him in the earnest hope that He will answer his prayer by granting him a perfect cure. We should prove our thankfulness to God for the good health which He has granted us, by helping to ease those who are stricken with illness.

It is our duty to seek reasons for pardoning the weaknesses which we discover in any person.

By doing our utmost to assist those in need, and consoling those who are in trouble of any kind, we are performing the will of our Heavenly Father; and we then practise the same laws of love and charity which He performs towards us His children.

## CHAPTER VIII

# PRAYER

PRAYER consists of expressions of heartfelt thanks and praise to the Living Everlasting God, our Heavenly Father; and the stating before Him of our daily needs. We come before Him with love and awe, and give utterance to our fears and anxieties, in the hope that He, in His great mercy, will grant us a perfect and speedy deliverance. Every minute, nay every second, of our lives we are in the utmost need of His care and help, and He is therefore ever ready to receive our prayers. By praying daily, we show our love for God; our thankfulness towards Him for His continued care and help, and our earnest desire to praise His holy name; but if we only pray to Him when we are in trouble, then it is obvious that we turn to Him not because we desire to express our feelings towards Him, but because we require His help and deliverance.

During the time that we offer our prayers, we face towards the east. When the building of the Temple had been completed, King Solomon recited beautiful prayers in it and requested God to accept all the prayers which would be said facing towards that Temple. Although that holy building is now destroyed, yet we offer our prayers towards the place where it once stood and earnestly hope that God will still accept them with additional favour.

Our prayers should not be said in a mere mechanical manner, but with all our hearts and minds. The Bible informs us that when the Israelites were groaning under the Egyptian slavery, they prayed to God for help and deliverance, and the All-knowing God granted to them their request, because He knew that they had pleaded before Him with all their hearts and minds. He found them worthy of His help because they had not recited their prayers merely with their lips, and permitted their minds to wander to other matters.

If we were standing before a king and requesting a favour of him, or discussing some matter with him, we would speak in a careful and serious manner; how much more, then, is it our duty to express our words in a slow, careful and earnest manner when we stand in prayer before God, who is the King of Kings, the Most Holy, blessed be He.

Consider how grateful we should be to our Heavenly Father for blessing us with life, good health, parents who love and cherish us, and many other things which make our lives happy and contented. We should realise our great dependence upon Him, and we shall then be filled to overflowing with feelings of gratitude and devotion, and we shall utter, with heartfelt earnestness, the words, ‘Blessed art thou, O Lord our God, King of the Universe, O God, our Father, our King, our Mighty One, our Creator, our Redeemer, our Maker, our Holy One, the Holy One of Jacob, our Shepherd, the Shepherd of Israel, O King, who art kind and dealest kindly with all, day by day thou hast dealt kindly, dost deal kindly, and wilt deal kindly with us: thou hast bestowed, thou dost bestow, thou wilt ever bestow benefits upon us, yielding us grace, loving-kindness, mercy and relief, deliverance and prosperity, blessing and salvation, consolation, sustenance and support, mercy, life, peace and all good: of no manner of good let us be in want.

‘The All-Merciful shall reign over us for ever and ever. The All-Merciful shall be blessed in heaven and on earth. The All-Merciful shall be praised throughout all generations, glorified amongst us to all eternity, and honoured amongst us for everlasting.’ This prayer should impress upon us the importance and need of beseeching at all times His assistance and care.

We must not only bless God for the good things which He grants us, but also for those things *which seem to us* to be against our good. When hearing good tidings, we say the blessing: ‘Blessed art thou, O Lord our God, King of the Universe, who is good and doest good’ (בָּרוּךְ אַתָּה יְיָ אֱלֹהֵינוּ מֶלֶךְ הָעוֹלָם · הַטּוֹב וְהַמֵּטִיב׃); and when hearing evil tidings, we say the blessing: ‘Blessed art thou, O Lord our God, King of the Universe, the true

Judge' (בָּרוּךְ אַתָּה יְיָ אֱלֹהֵינוּ מֶלֶךְ הָעוֹלָם · דַּיַּן הָאֱמֶת:). The very words which we say in these blessings prove to us that we believe that the Almighty God is the source of all things and happenings, and that all which He does is done for a definite purpose.

Let us therefore be ever ready to confide in Him, and talk to Him with as respectful a familiarity as we would speak to our earthly father. When we feel troubled and desire help, we may be assured that God is eager to help us, if we will only put our faith and hope in Him. We are permitted to pray in any pure place as the whole world is filled with the presence and glory of God.

## CHAPTER IX

# FAITH IN GOD

In the course of our lives we are very often anxious to obtain a certain thing, or that a certain event should, or should not, take place; but although we offer prayers before God to grant us His help, yet our desires remain unfulfilled, and very often we find that the contrary of our desires actually takes place. When such events occur, we are apt to become very sad, and our faith in God and power of prayer to become weakened. But we are very greatly mistaken, and the fact that such thoughts enter our minds is in itself a proof that we are not possessors of a deep-rooted faith in God and His power and mercy. If we truly trusted in Him we should realise that not only is He our Heavenly Father but also our continual Guardian, and that it is because He is our Guardian that He does not satisfy our every desire. Many of the things for which we pray would, if they were granted, prove of the utmost disadvantage to us; but as we have only been endowed with human intelligence, and are therefore unable to know what will happen in the future, we do not realise these future disadvantages. Nothing is hidden from our Heavenly Guardian, however, and He, therefore, only grants us those of our requests which will prove to our advantage.

During the years of our lives many events take place for which we find it impossible to discover a reason. It may be that a very good religious person is seen to suffer great pain or hunger; or a child is suddenly killed; or some other event takes place for which we cannot account, and we begin to wonder that God, in His great mercy, should permit such events to happen. When such events or incidents do occur, then we should realise that God would not have permitted them unless there was a great and important purpose to be served thereby.

In order better to understand the care and guardianship which God showers upon those who trust in Him, let us read an incident in the life of a very learned Rabbi, called Akiba. This Rabbi was compelled to leave his native land and wander about from place to place, as the learned and pious Jews were being punished in that land because of their continued obedience to God and the Torah. Notwithstanding the great suffering which he was forced to undergo, Akiba retained a wholehearted faith in God, and firmly believed that all He did was done for the best. All he possessed was a lamp by which he studied at night, a cock which roused him at the time of dawn, and an ass upon which he rode. Feeling much fatigued, he arrived at a village and requested to be permitted to remain there until the next morning; but the people were very cruel and would not grant his request, and he was therefore compelled to seek shelter in a neighbouring wood. After making himself as comfortable as was possible, he lit his lamp and commenced to study, but a strong gust of wind extinguished the light, and he exclaimed: 'Am I even to be deprived of the pleasure of study; yet God is just, and whatsoever He does is for the best.' A few hours later a fierce wolf killed the cock, and so he exclaimed: 'What new trouble is this, and who will now rouse me to the study of the Torah? But God is just, and whatsoever He does is for the best.' Scarcely had he had sufficient time to reconcile himself to his losses when a lion attacked and killed his ass, and he then exclaimed: 'Whatever can I do now? The lamp and the cock have been taken from me, and now the poor ass is also gone! Yet, praised be the Lord, whatsoever He does is for the best.' After passing sleepless hours, he returned to the village where he had called the previous night, and was greatly surprised at being unable to discover a single living person there. A band of robbers had entered the village and, after killing the inhabitants, had taken their possessions. As soon as he had overcome his surprise, he raised his voice in praise to God, and said: 'Thou great God, the God of Abraham, Isaac and Jacob, now I know by experience that poor human beings are indeed short-sighted, and often mistake what you do for their good, as something which is against their good. But thou alone art just, and kind, and merciful! Had not the hard-hearted people driven me from the village, I should also have shared their fate; had not the wind put out my lamp, the robbers would have been drawn to my resting place and would have killed me; it was also thy great mercy which was the cause of the loss of the cock and the ass, that they might not, by their noise, give notice of the place where I was. Praised, then, be Thy Holy Name for ever and ever ! '

This experience of Rabbi Akiba should teach us to be firmly convinced of the merciful guardianship of God; and that even if He causes things to take place which we find painful or difficult to bear, yet we should trust in Him and be convinced that they are caused for a definite purpose and for our good. We should continually be prepared to say, like Rabbi Akiba, that ' God is just, and whatsoever He does is for the best '.

## CHAPTER X

# MORAL DUTIES

THERE are certain duties the fulfilment of which is fundamentally necessary in order that we may be capable of living at peace with our God, and with our neighbours. Every person, whether he is a Jew or a member of some other religion, must, to some extent, fulfil these duties; but we, who are the chosen people of God, have a much greater responsibility than other people, as we must cause our actions to serve as examples to them. Let us therefore read of these duties, and do our utmost to fulfil that which they require us to do or believe.

### OUR DUTIES TO GOD

These duties require that we should fear, love and serve Him. To fear God does not only mean that we must fear to sin because of the punishment which will follow, but that we must be filled with fear and respect when we consider how tremendous, good and merciful He is, whilst we are so puny and unimportant when compared with Him. These thoughts will lead us to obey His laws and commandments with willing hearts, in order that we may be, to some small degree, worthy of the care and notice which He, in His love, takes of us. We will always do our utmost to deserve that love, and we will only feel happy when we possess it; we will serve Him by continually being careful and painstaking in the performance of our religious duties, and will not permit anything to hinder our fulfilment of them. We will sing His praises, and will confide in Him by means of prayer, firmly believing that He, in His great mercy, will listen to us and will guard us from all manner of serious hurt. As we are merely human, it is natural for us to commit actions which are not pleasing before Him, but feelings of heartfelt regret should immediately follow such actions, and we must promise to guard ourselves, as much as is humanly possible, from repeating them. That confession and true repentance is acceptable before God is proved by the words: 'I admitted my sin unto Thee, and mine iniquity have I not hid; I said I will make confession about my transgressions unto the Lord, and Thou, Thou forgavest the iniquity of my sins, Selah' (Psalms, xxxii, 5).

## Duties Towards our Neighbours

Our religion impresses upon us the duties which we owe towards the poor, the orphan, the widow, and our neighbours. The word 'neighbours' does not only mean the persons who live near us, but any persons with whom we come in contact, or to whom we can show sympathy and consideration. These duties should teach us to practise love, justice and charity towards one another.

We show our love to our neighbour by trying at all times to appreciate his good qualities and excusing his faults; by considering his welfare as important as our own; and by doing all which is in our power to prevent harm from befalling him. We should feel glad when he is happy and sympathise with him when he is sad or troubled. These feelings of love will lead us to deal justly with him, and will guard us from wronging or injuring him in any possible manner; we will not bear a grudge against him, or harbour feelings of anger, hatred, revenge or jealousy towards him, as it is written: ‘ Thou shalt not go up and down as a tale-bearer among thy people; neither shalt thou stand against the blood of thy neighbour; I am the Lord. Thou shalt not hate thy brother in thine heart; thou shalt not in any wise rebuke thy neighbour, and not suffer sin upon him. Thou shalt not avenge nor bear any grudge against the children of thy people, but thou shalt love thy neighbour as thyself; I am the Lord’ (Leviticus, xix, 16-18). If our neighbour is unfriendly towards us, or ill-uses us in any manner, we are not permitted to make this an excuse for neglecting to fulfil our duty towards him. We should defend him against the slander of other people, and from their efforts to injure his character.

Consider the wonderful happiness with which the

world would be filled if we all united in brotherly love, and sought the welfare of one another.

## Our Duties Towards Other People

That we should have duties towards our parents is not at all surprising, as if we consider the love and care which they have bestowed upon us since the time we came into this world in a state of utter helplessness, then we shall understand the great debt of gratitude which we owe them, and how much it is our duty to love, honour and guard them now that we are able to do so. The aged and learned benefit us by their experience and knowledge, and it is therefore our duty to be respectful, obedient and humble towards them. We should treat with kindness and consideration those who are younger or less intelligent than ourselves; and cause our actions to serve as good examples for them. These duties have been taught us in the words of Rabbi Ishmael: ' Be obedient and humble towards your superiors; agreeable in all ways towards your inferiors, and receive all men with cheerfulness ' (*Ethics of the Fathers*, Chap. III).

## Our Duties Towards Animals

Although we are taught in the Bible that after God had created the animal kingdom he appointed man to rule over it, as it is written: ' Let us make man in our image, after our likeness; and let them have absolute rule over the fish of the sea, and over the birds of the air, and over the cattle, and over all the earth, and over every creeping thing that creepeth upon the earth' (Genesis, i, 26), yet we are commanded certain duties towards them which are intended to safeguard them against pain or cruel treatment. In addition to those duties towards them which have been mentioned in Genesis (chapter xxiv), we are also commanded to grant them rest on the Sabbath day; and that we should not cause a weak animal to work together with a strong one, by fastening them together, as the strain will be too great for the weaker animal. We are forbidden to muzzle an animal when it is working on a field of corn or hay, as it will suffer pain because of its inability to satisfy the desire to eat of the corn or hay. We must assist any animal whose burden is too heavy for it to bear, or in any other manner in which it may need our assistance. We must satisfy its hunger and thirst; provide for its comfort; and attend to any other necessities which it may require.

The duty of saving birds from pain is the intention of the command: 'If a bird's nest chance to be before thee on the way, in any tree or on the ground, whether they be young ones or eggs, and the mother sitting upon the young or upon the eggs; thou shalt not take the mother with the young' (Deuteronomy, xxii, 6).

CHAPTER XI

# THE THIRTEEN PRINCIPLES OF FAITH

Among the famous Rabbis who have shed lustre upon the Jewish name there is one whose name was Moses, the son of Maimon, or as he was later called, Maimonides. In order to help those Jews who desired to live according to the law of the Torah, but found it too complicated in its original and final form, he set himself the task of simplifying it by adding an explanation or commentary. In one of his commentaries he informs us that there are thirteen main beliefs, or principles, of faith, which it is essential for us to accept if we desire to remain true and faithful followers of the Jewish religion. Later Rabbis disputed these principles and wished to lessen their number, but the teachings of Maimonides prevailed, and were universally accepted. They were inserted in the Prayer Book both in their original form, which is known in Hebrew as :שְׁלֹשָׁה עָשָׂר עִקָּרִים, and in a metric version well known as 'Yigdal' (יִגְדַּל) from its first word. The first five principles deal with the belief in the existence of God; the next four deal with the belief that Biblical Revelation was from God; and the last four deal with the belief in divine reward and punishment. We will now read about them, and learn the lessons which they contain.

## The First Principle

*I believe with perfect faith that the Creator, blessed be His name, is the Author and Guide of everything that has been created, and that He alone has made, does make, and will make all things.*

This principle teaches us that we must firmly believe in the existence of God, as Creator of all things, as it is written: ' By the word of the Lord the heavens were made, and by the breath of His mouth all their host ' (Psalm xxxiii, 6). It also teaches us that when God had created all things, He did not leave them to themselves, but continued, and still continues, to preside over them; taking wise and kind care of all His works, and directing them so wonderfully, that nothing happens by chance. The words, ' Has made, does make, and will make all things ', teach us that as no other than God can create anything, therefore all creations, whether past, present or future, must come from God Himself, as it is written: ' I have made the earth, and created man upon it: I, even my hands, have stretched out the heavens, and all their host have I commanded ' (Isaiah, xlv, 12). His powers are unlimited, and no other power has, does, or will exist to help Him in His work. The laws of nature should be a proof to us of the workings of the wise and powerful Ruler. The great world in which we live, with all its wonderful creatures, its beautiful flowers and other creations, are all under the ever-watchful care of God, who created them and attends to them in all their needs. Our own existence is due to the Creator of the whole world, and He it is who supports us and cares for us at all times.

## The Second Principle

*I believe with perfect faith that the Creator, blessed be His name, is a Unity, and that there is no unity in any manner like unto His, and that He alone is our God, who was, is, and will be.*

This principle teaches us that we must firmly believe that the Almighty God is the One supreme power, and that there is none other beside Him, as it is written: 'Know thou, this day, and consider in thy heart, that the Eternal is God in heaven above, and on the earth beneath, there is none else' (Deuteronomy, iv, 39). It is not enough for us to only believe that there is One God, but we must understand that He cannot be separated into parts. In every generation the Jewish people have, three times daily, expressed the belief in the Unity of God with the words: 'Hear, O Israel, the Lord our God, the Lord is One' (Deuteronomy, vi, 4); they gave up their lives for this belief, and willingly suffered great tortures rather than deny it. The words, 'There is no Unity like unto His', should teach us that beside God nothing exists which is not made up of several parts; He, therefore, is the only existence which can be termed a perfect Unity, having no parts whatsoever. There are millions of people who agree that God is One, but they add that His Oneness is made up of three separate powers who are united; each power having a special quality and purpose. Such beliefs are absolutely denied by members of the Jewish nation, as they are contrary to the teachings of their religion.

## The Third Principle

*I believe with perfect faith that the Creator, blessed be His name, is not a body, and that He is free from all the accidents of matter, and that He has not any form whatsoever.*

This principle teaches us that we must firmly believe that God has no form, shape or figure, and that He therefore cannot die or suffer any of the changes to which human beings or matter are liable. As He does not possess a form, it is impossible for any living person to see him; and we are therefore strictly forbidden to imagine any kind of picture of Him. The impossibility of forming any manner of imaginary likeness of Him is expressed in the words: ' To whom then will ye liken Me, or shall I be equal, saith the Holy One ' (Isaiah, xl, 25); or again in the words: ' Take ye, therefore, good heed unto yourselves, for ye saw no manner of likeness on the day that the Lord spake unto you in Horeb out of the midst of the fire. Lest you corrupt yourselves, and make yourselves a graven image, the likeness of any figure, the likeness of male or female. The likeness of any beast that is on the earth, the likeness of any winged fowl that flieth in the air. The likeness of anything that creepeth on the ground, the likeness of any fish that is in the water beneath the earth' (Deuteronomy, iv, 15-18). God is a Spirit, and they who worship Him must do so with all their spirit or mind. We have read in the Bible of the 'Mighty Hand of God', or the 'Outstretched arm of God', or other such sayings which might lead us to think that God is possessed of bodily organs; but these words are not meant to convey such meanings, but must be understood in a figurative manner. If we discuss a matter with an adult, and later discuss the same matter with a child, we shall most certainly talk to the one in a different manner from the way in which we talk to the other. When talking to the child *we will use such words as will best help it to understand exactly that which we desire it to know*. We are all children of One Heavenly Father, but, unlike Him, we possess a form and bodily organs; and when, therefore, we are to understand His great power, we are figuratively told of His Mighty Hand. In a like manner, figurative speech is used whenever we are informed of an attribute of God which we should otherwise be unable to comprehend. It is beyond human powers to grasp, for example, how God, having no bodily organs or form of any kind, could have created the world and all that it contains; or is able to watch and guard over all His works; or was capable of performing the miracles which are described in the Bible; or is capable of performing actions of any kind. For this reason, our

Rabbis inform us, whenever it was necessary for such actions to be mentioned in the Bible, it became essential to describe them in the language which is used when describing the actions of a human being; and in this way we have been able to form an idea of things which would otherwise have been far beyond our human, and therefore limited, comprehension.

## The Fourth Principle

*I believe with perfect faith that the Creator, blessed be His name, is the first and will be the last.*

This principle teaches us that we must firmly believe that God existed before anything or anyone else, and that He will continue to exist when everything and everyone else will have come to an end. Believing as we do that He created all, and that He cares for and governs all which He has created, it is quite simple to understand that He must have been before all, and must continue to be after all has ended.

This existence of God before all is taught by the words: 'Before the mountains were brought forth, or ever thou hadst formed the earth and the world, even from everlasting to everlasting, Thou art God' (Psalm xc, 2); whilst His continued existence after all is taught by the words: 'They shall perish, but Thou shalt endure; yea, all of them shall wax old like a garment; as a vesture shalt Thou change them, and they shall pass away. But Thou art the selfsame, and Thy years shall have no end' (Psalm cii, 27, 28).

## CHAPTER XII

# PRINCIPLES OF FAITH (*continued*)

### The Fifth Principle

*I believe with perfect faith that to the Creator, blessed be His name, and to Him alone, it is right to pray, and that it is not right to pray to any being beside Him.*

This principle teaches us that we must firmly believe that it is our duty to pray to our Heavenly Father, the Merciful God. We should express, through words of prayer, our heartfelt thanks to Him for all His great benefits towards us; and also express our needs to Him, as the gracious giver of all things, as it is written: 'The eyes of all wait upon Thee; and Thou givest them their food in due season. Thou openest thine hand, and satisfiest every living thing with favour' (Psalm cxlv, 15, 16). We should highly praise Him, hoping in Him at all times, and realising that He is gracious, merciful and slow to anger; as only by realising, and firmly believing, that He possesses these qualities, are we able to put our sincere faith in Him. 'The Lord is gracious, and full of compassion; slow to anger, and of great mercy. The Lord is good to all; and His tender mercies are over all His works' (Psalm cxlv, 8, 9).

The words 'and that it is not right to pray to any

being besides Him ', express one of the fundamental differences between the Jewish and other religions of the world. The people of other religions firmly believe that there are holy spirits to whom they are able to pray, and that these spirits intercede on their behalf and obtain forgiveness for them from God. The Jewish religion teaches the Jew, however, that it is both sinful and useless for him to pray to any spirits; but that God is Himself at all times ready to listen to our sincere prayers, and the assistance of spirits is not required. 'The Lord is nigh unto all them that call upon Him, to all that call upon Him in truth (sincerely). He will fulfil the desire of them that fear Him; He also will hear their cry, and will save them' (Psalm cxlv, 18, 19). That no power can deliver us from that which He has decided for us, is taught by the words: 'See now that I, even I, am He, and there is no God with me; I kill, and I make alive; I have wounded, and I heal; *and there is none* that can deliver out of my hand' (Deuteronomy, xxxii, 39). Our continual trust, therefore, should be in Him, and in no other than Him.

## The Sixth Principle

*I believe with perfect faith that all the words of the prophets are true.*

This principle teaches us that we must firmly believe that the words spoken by the prophets to the people, and which were written down in the Bible, had been received by them from God. At certain times He made His messages known to the people through His messengers, who were called Prophets. These prophets were pious persons who, although they were human beings, possessed spiritual powers to an exceptional degree, and became, during the time in which they were delivering God's message, controlled by the direct influence of God. These messages were received by the prophet from God during a dream or vision, as it is written: 'And He said: Hear now my words; if there be a prophet amongst you, I, the Lord, will make Myself known unto him in a vision. I will speak with him in a dream' (Numbers, xii, 6). The messages were usually threats of punishment for wrong-doing, but very often consisted of words of comfort and hope.

There were undoubtedly many false prophets who delivered messages, and untruthfully claimed them to have come from God, and for this reason the Bible issued the warning, 'When a prophet speaketh in the name of the Lord, if the thing follow not, nor come to pass, that is the thing which the Lord hath not spoken; the prophet hath spoken it presumptuously, thou shalt not be afraid of him' (Deuteronomy, xviii, 22). The messages which were delivered by the true prophets were, at a later date, fulfilled, and were thus proved to have come from God. All the words of the prophets which are contained in the Bible are referred to in this principle of faith.

## The Seventh Principle

*I believe with perfect faith that the prophecy of Moses, our teacher, peace be unto him, was true, and that he was the chief of the prophets, both of those that were before him, and those that followed him.*

This principle teaches us that we must firmly believe that Moses was the greatest prophet that has ever existed, and that the Law which was given through him is the true will of God. He is called the 'chief of the prophets' because he was the only one to whom God spoke face to face, as it is written: 'And there arose not a prophet since in Israel like unto Moses, whom the Lord knew face to face' (Deuteronomy, xxxiv, 10). To the other prophets God spoke only in a dream or vision, but Moses heard the Divine voice speaking to him while he was fully awake, as it is written: 'My servant Moses is not so (as other prophets), who is faithful in all mine house. With him will I speak mouth to mouth, even apparently, and not in dark speeches' (Numbers, xii, 7, 8). Another reason for considering Moses the greatest prophet is that it was he who was entrusted by God to deliver His greatest message, the Ten Commandments, as it is written: 'And the Lord said unto Moses, come up to me into the mount, and be there, and I will give thee tables of stone, and a Law, and commandments which I have written; that thou mayest teach them' (Exodus, xxiv, 12); this message served as a guide of life to persons in every generation, but the messages of other prophets were only suitable for the time in which they were delivered. The greatness of Moses is yet further described to us by the words: ' In all the signs and the wonders which the Lord sent him to do in the land of Egypt to Pharaoh, and to all his servants, and to all his land. And in all that mighty hands, and in all the terror which Moses shewed in the sight of Israel' (Deuteronomy, xxxiv, 11, 12).

The words ' face to face ' do not mean that Moses saw the face of God, as we have already read that He has no body, figure or form; but they signify that Moses was nearer to God at the time when he ascended Mount Sinai to receive the Commandments than any other living person has or ever will be; as only a cloud separated them.

## The Eighth Principle

*I believe with perfect faith that the whole Law, now in our possession, is the same that was given to Moses our teacher, peace be unto him.*

This principle teaches us that we must firmly believe that the Torah, or Law, which we still cherish as a treasure from God, is the same Torah which He gave to Moses on Mount Sinai. We know that it has not been changed, because it has been guarded most preciously in all generations, and has not left our possession even during the times when the people of other religions tortured us for remaining true to its demands.

The words, ' the whole of the Law ', are meant to include both the ' Written Law ' (תּוֹרָה שֶׁבִּכְתָב) and the ' Oral Law ' (תּוֹרָה שֶׁבְּעַל פֶּה). The Written Law is the name given to the Five Books of Moses, which were written by him at the command of God, and which contain the precepts of the Law revealed to him on the Mount. The Oral Law is the name given to the traditional explanation of the Written Law which Moses taught by word of mouth, and which was handed down by word of mouth from one generation to another, until it became necessary for its preservation that it should be put in writing: ' Moses received the Law from Sinai, and delivered it to Joshua, and Joshua to the elders, and the elders to the prophets, and the prophets to the men of the Great Synagogue ' (*Ethics of the Fathers*, i, 1). These writings of the Oral Law were called ' Mishnah ' (מִשְׁנָה), and were later more fully explained, the explanations being called ' Talmud ' or ' Gemorah ' (גְּמָרָא). The Oral Law is essential for the correct understanding of the Written Law; as it teaches us, for example, exactly what is forbidden as work on the Sabbath day; the exact manner in which we should slaughter our animals or birds, so that they should be spared from pain; the things we are permitted or forbidden to do during festivals; and many other such matters which are of the utmost importance if we desire to know how correctly to fulfil that which we have been commanded in the Written Law.

The eighth principle, therefore, teaches us that both the Written and Oral Laws must be accepted as having been given to Moses on Mount Sinai.

### The Ninth Principle

*I believe with perfect faith that this Law will not be changed, and that there will never be any other Law from the Creator, blessed be His name.*

This principle teaches us that we must firmly believe that, like its author, the Law is eternal and unchangeable, as it is written: ' As for me, this is my covenant with them, saith the Lord; my spirit that is upon thee, and my words which I have put in thy mouth, shall not depart out of thy mouth, nor out of the mouth of thy seed, nor out of the mouth of thy seed's seed, saith the Lord, from henceforth and for ever ' (Isaiah, lix, 21).

This is another of the chief differences between the Jew and the people of other religions. They believe that many of the Laws which God gave to Moses have since been changed by Him, and that He has revealed the alterations to the founders of their respective religions; but the Jew is quite unable to accept these beliefs; he knows that the Law which God once gave was given for all times, as the Everlasting God does not change His mind. Another proof that the Law of Moses has not been changed is to be found in the fact that at the time when God desired to give us the Law He assembled all Israel at the foot of Mount Sinai, and delivered it amidst thunder, lightning and great wonders, as it is written: 'And the Lord said unto Moses, Lo, I come unto thee in a thick cloud, that the people may hear when I speak with thee, and may also believe thee for ever' (Exodus, xix, 9). If, therefore, He later desired to make any alteration in this Law, He would most certainly have done so quite as publicly, and not in private to a single person.

## CHAPTER XIII

# PRINCIPLES OF FAITH (*continued*)

### The Tenth Principle

*I believe with perfect faith that the Creator, blessed be His name, knows every deed of the children of men, and all their thoughts, as it is said : 'It is He that fashioneth the hearts of them all, that giveth heed to all their deeds.'*

This principle teaches us that we must firmly believe that God knows and observes our every thought and action, and that it is quite impossible to keep anything hidden from Him. We should therefore strive to make every word, thought or action to be pleasing before Him.

He is not possessed of human organs but is entirely spirit, and is therefore capable of seeing the actions, and knowing the thoughts, of all people at the same time. That He is Omniscient is taught us by the words: 'He formeth their hearts together, He is acquainted with all their deeds' (Psalm xxxiii, 15); and His Omnipresence is taught us by the words: 'Whither shall I go from Thy spirit? Or whither shall I flee from Thy presence? If I ascend up into heaven, Thou art there. If I make my bed in the nether-world, behold, Thou art there. If I take the wings of the morning, and dwell in the uttermost parts of the sea; even there would Thy hand lead me, and Thy right hand would hold me. And if I say: " Surely the darkness shall envelop me, and the light about me shall be night ", even the darkness is not too dark for Thee, but the night shineth as the day; the darkness is even as the light ' (Psalm cxxxix, 7-12).

## The Eleventh Principle

*I believe with perfect faith that the Creator, blessed be His name, rewards those that keep His commandments, and punishes those that transgress them.*

This principle teaches us that we must firmly believe that God will reward or punish us according to our actions in life. Some persons are rewarded or punished whilst they are yet alive; others, after this life, when the soul returns to God and has to account for the actions which it has performed during the time which it spent in this world. The body is unable to do anything without being directed by the soul, and so it is the soul which is held to be responsible for our actions. We read in the Bible that God punished or rewarded people according to their actions; but this should not cause us to give up hope of forgiveness, or faith in His mercy; we cannot escape from His justice, but we can obtain His pardon, through *true* repentance. One of our Rabbis has said that we should repent one day before our death; and as we do not know when will be the day of death, it therefore becomes our duty to repent each day of our lives, as perhaps that day will be our last. The doctrine of the reward and punishment of mankind is clearly expressed in the words: 'Say to the righteous that they shall have good, for they shall eat the fruit of their doings. Woe unto the wicked, for he shall have evil, for the reward of his hands shall be given to him' (Isaiah, iii, 10, 11). That we are, to some extent, rewarded or punished during the years of our lives, is expressed in the words: 'Behold, the righteous shall be recompensed in the earth, much more the wicked and the sinner' (Proverbs, xi, 31).

## The Twelfth Principle

*I believe with perfect faith in the coming of the Messiah, and, though he tarry, I will wait daily for his coming.*

This principle teaches us that we must firmly believe that when the proper time will have arrived God will send a human being, who will be called a 'Messiah' (מָשִׁיחַ), which means 'Anointed', and will be a descendant of King David, to lead the Jewish people back to their own land, the land of Israel; as it is written: 'And it shall come to pass in that day, that the root of Jesse, which standeth for a banner of the peoples, unto him shall the nations seek; and his resting place shall be glorious. And it shall come to pass in that day, that the Lord shall set His hand again the second time to recover the remnant of His people. And He shall set up a banner for the nations, and shall assemble the outcasts of Israel, and gather together the scattered of Judah from the four corners of the earth' (Isaiah, xi, 10-12).

The Messiah will also be the cause of all nations joining together in praise of the One and only True God, as it is written: 'And the Lord shall be King over all the earth; in that day shall the Lord be One, and His name One' (Zechariah, xiv, 9).

All mankind will live at peace with one another, and wars will be ended for ever, as it is written: 'And they shall beat their swords into plough-shares, and their spears into pruning hooks: Nation shall not lift up sword against nation, neither shall they learn war any more. But they shall sit every man under his vine and under his fig-tree; and none shall make them afraid' (Micah, iv, 3, 4).

We are quite unaware when this Messiah will come, but we can hasten his arrival by obeying the Laws and Commandments of God, and by proving ourselves worthy of his coming. He will be recognised by certain signs; as we are told that God will send the prophet Elijah to inform us of the forthcoming event, as it is written: 'Behold, I will send you Elijah the prophet before the great and terrible day of the Lord come' (Malachi, iv, 5); and we are also told that the Spirit of God will rest upon him, as it is written: 'And the Spirit of the Lord will rest upon him, the spirit of wisdom and understanding, the spirit of counsel and might, the spirit of knowledge and of fear of the Lord' (Isaiah, xi, 2).

The prayer read at the conclusion of each of the three daily services contains, in its second portion, a beautiful picture of the world in the days of the Messiah. It reads as follows: 'We therefore hope in Thee, O Lord our God, that we may speedily behold the glory of Thy might, when Thou wilt remove the abominations from the earth, and the idols will be utterly cut off, when the world will be perfected under the kingdom of the Almighty, and all the children of flesh will call upon Thy name, when Thou wilt turn unto Thyself all the wicked of the earth. Let all the inhabitants of the world perceive and know that unto Thee every knee must bow, every tongue must swear. Before Thee, O Lord our God, let them bow and fall; and unto Thy glorious name let them give honour; let them all accept the yoke of Thy kingdom, and do Thou reign over them speedily, and for ever and ever. For the kingdom is Thine and to all eternity Thou wilt reign in glory; as it is written in Thy Law: "The Lord shall reign for ever and ever." And it is said: "And the Lord shall be King over all the earth; in that day shall the Lord be One, and His name One".'

## The Thirteenth Principle

*I believe with perfect faith that there will be a resurrection of the dead at the time when it shall please the Creator, blessed be His name, and exalted be the remembrance of Him for ever and ever.*

This principle teaches us that we must firmly believe that God will, at the time of the coming of the Messiah, bring to life again those persons who have died. We, who are the possessors of only a limited intellect, are unable to comprehend what will actually take place, or how this miracle will be performed. A disbeliever once said to a Rabbi: ' You are fools, who believe in a resurrection of the dead ! Do you not see that living persons die ? How then can you believe that the dead shall again live ? ' ' Foolish man ! ' replied the Rabbi. ' You believe in a creation; well, then, if what never before existed, exists, why may not that which once existed, exist again ? '

We read in the Bible that the Creator formed a figure of a man from dust, and then breathed a breath of life into his nostrils; this breath of life (נִשְׁמַת חַיִּים) is called a Soul. 'And the Lord God formed man of the dust of the ground, and breathed into his nostrils the breath of life; and man became a living soul ' (Genesis, ii, 7).

When a person dies, the body is buried in the earth, but the soul returns to God; as it is the breath of God, and therefore as part of Himself, it cannot die. It is this Soul that the principle teaches us to believe will be again united with the body at the time of the resurrection, and that therefore the dead will again live.

CHAPTER XIV

# THE THREE OUTWARD SIGNS

IN THE first portion of the Shema we are commanded to bind the words of God upon our hands and between our eyes, and to write them upon our doorposts; in the last portion we are commanded to fasten fringes to our garments.

## THE TEPHILLIN (תְּפִלִּין)

The Command to bind the words of God upon our hands and between our eyes is to be found in four places, or paragraphs, in the Torah, and in order to fulfil this command we fasten a special leather case to the left arm, so that it rests opposite the heart. This case is fastened to the arm by means of a leather strap called a רְצוּעָה, and contains a piece of parchment upon which the four paragraphs have been written. We next fasten a similar case to the front of the head, so that it lies just above the forehead and between the eyes. This case is also fastened by means of a רְצוּעָה, and contains four pieces of parchment upon each of which a different paragraph has been written. These cases are called בָּתִּים, and when the parchment has been enclosed they are called תְּפִלִּין ('Tephillin' or 'Phylacteries'). The Tephillah of the hand (תְּפִלִּין שֶׁל יָד) is put on before the Tephillah of the head (תְּפִלִּין שֶׁל ראשׁ), because we are first commanded to bind them on the hand; but when they are being removed, the opposite order is observed.

Each of the biblical paragraphs contained in the בָּתִּים has a special lesson to teach us. In one paragraph we are commanded קַדֶּשׁ לִי כָל בְּכוֹר: 'Sanctify unto me all the first-born', etc. (Exodus, xiii, 1-10). It is the first-born child who is most treasured, and as we have been chosen by God as His Treasured People (עַם סְגֻלָּה) we are therefore also regarded by Him as His first-born children. It is thus our duty, as God's first-born children, to cause our lives to be filled with good deeds and pure thoughts; in order that we should be sanctified before Him. The paragraph which commences with the words וְהָיָה כִּי יְבִאֲךָ 'And it shall be when the Eternal shall bring thee', etc. (Exodus, xiii, 11-16), should also teach us the necessity of living pure and holy lives; and should remind us that the Almighty God released our forefathers from the Egyptian slavery, and, by leading them into Canaan, fulfilled the promise He had made to Abraham.

We will then be reminded that He has also promised to lead us back to our own land, at a time when He will know that we are sufficiently prepared for the great event; and we should eagerly await the fulfilment of this promise. The paragraph which consists of the first portion of the Shema (Deuteronomy, vi, 4-9) should teach us that the Lord our God is One; that it is our duty to love and serve Him at all times;

and that we should spread, both by word and action, a knowledge of His Torah. The paragraph which consists of the second portion of the Shema (Deuteronomy, xi, 13-21), should teach us to remain faithful to our God, and that our reward or punishment depends upon ourselves.

We do not fulfil the purpose of the command to bind the words of God upon our hands and between our eyes if we merely fasten them without bearing in mind the important lessons which they are intended to teach us. These lessons, if we permit them to influence our thoughts and desires, will not only remind us to be good and conscientious Jews at all times, but also that the desires of our hearts (which are facing the Tephillah on the arm), the thoughts of our minds and visions of our eyes (the head Tephillah rests on the forehead betweed the eyes), must be pure, and directed to the love and service of God, our Heavenly Father.

The Tephillin are not worn by females, or by males who have not yet reached the age of thirteen years and one day. As Sabbaths and Festivals are themselves reminders of God, and serve as signs between Him and the Jewish people, it becomes unnecessary for us to wear them on those days.

## The Mezuzah (מְזוּזָה)

In order to fulfil the command of writing the words of God upon our doorposts, the first two portions of the Shema are written upon a piece of parchment, which is then folded and put into a special case, and is then called a Mezuzah (meaning 'doorpost'). On the other side of the parchment the word שַׁדַּי, 'Almighty' is written, and either a slit is made in the case through which this word can be seen or the word is also impressed on the case itself. This Mezuzah is then fixed on the right-hand doorposts of the entrances to our houses or rooms, and should serve as reminders that the care and love of God is continually watching over us and guarding us from all harm. The word שַׁדַּי should remind us of the power of the Almighty God, and that we have no cause to fear any human being as long as we put our heartfelt hope and trust in Him. When passing a Mezuzah we should touch it at the word שַׁדַּי, and kiss that with which we have touched it.

An emperor once sent a very valuable gift to a Rabbi as a sign of his friendship, and received, in return, the gift of a Mezuzah. The emperor was greatly surprised and said, when he next met the Rabbi: 'The present which I sent to you was of very much greater value than that which you sent to me in return.' The Rabbi replied: 'Over your present I must watch and guard as otherwise it is liable to be stolen or lost; but my present will watch and guard over you, and protect you from all harm.'

Many people seem ashamed of their religion, and so they fasten the Mezuzah on the inside of their doorways, where strangers cannot see it, and will therefore be unaware that they are Jews. This is very wrong indeed, as we should always feel honoured to belong to a people with so distinguished a record as the Jews. We should fasten the Mezuzah *outside* our doorways, and in this way we shall make known that our homes are secure in the guardianship of God, whose strength and might fills the world.

## The Fringes (צִיצִית)

In order to fulfil the precept of the Fringes, we fasten them to a special garment which is worn underneath the outer garments, and because it has four corners it is called an אַרְבַּע כַּנְפוֹת (' Arbah Kanfos '), which means ' four corners '. These Fringes are made by doubling four threads of wool or silk, one of which is then wound around the others seven, eight, eleven and thirteen times, a double-knot being made between each set of windings. We then have eight threads and five double-knots. If two of these threads are torn off, or missing, the Fringes become unsuitable for use.

We are told in the third portion of the Shema that when we see the Fringes we shall remember *all the Commandments of God*. To understand the meaning which underlies these words we must remember that the Jewish religion contains six hundred and thirteen commandments. In Hebrew the letter צ stands for the number ninety; the letter י stands for the number ten; and the letter ת stands for the number four hundred. The word צִיצִית, therefore, stands for the number six hundred, and if we add the eight strings and five double-knots, we get the number six hundred and thirteen. When we look at the Fringes we are reminded of the number six hundred and thirteen, and this in turn reminds us of the six hundred and thirteen commandments of our religion. Many of these commandments cannot be obeyed at the present time, as they deal with the offering of sacrifices, sowing and reaping of fields, and other such matters which could only be carried out when we possessed our land and our Temple. We should take great care, however, not merely to remember the commandments of God but to do our utmost to obey and honour them, and by ever bearing them in mind keep ourselves far from sinful actions and thoughts, at all times and in all places.

## CHAPTER XV

# THE DIETARY LAWS

THE Bible contains Laws which permit or forbid us to eat certain kinds of foods. God has not forbidden these foods merely because He does not wish us to enjoy them, as He is our merciful Father who desires us to enjoy our lives and be happy and contented, but He has chosen us as His special people, and He, therefore, desires us to remain a holy nation. For this reason He has commanded: ' And ye shall be holy unto me; for I, the Lord, am holy, and have separated you from other people, that ye should be mine ' (Leviticus, xx, 26).

God, as you have just read, does not wish us to join too intimately with the people of other religions, as they have different beliefs and different standards of conduct. Eating together at the same table is one of the best ways of creating friendships. By being forbidden, therefore, to eat certain foods, we are kept from joining with them during meals, and in this way becoming as familiar with them as would otherwise be the case, and in this way being led astray from the true worship of God.

Because Jews, in every generation, have obeyed these Laws, we are still a nation, and can continue to practise and keep alive that beautiful religion which it is our privilege to possess. If these laws had not been obeyed, we would have gradually joined in close friendship with the peoples of other nations; we would have married with their sons and daughters, our religion would have gravely suffered, and our nation would have therefore been in great danger of becoming assimilated amongst the other nations of the world. We must not think, however, that because we are forbidden to join with the people of other religions we are also forbidden to be friendly with them; our God is the merciful Father of all people, and He does not desire us to be unfriendly with each other. We must do all in our power to help and sympathise with one another, but we should not permit the friendship which exists between us to become so intimate that it will lead us, in any manner, to disobey the laws and commandments of our own religion.

Another reason for these dietary laws is, that the animals, birds or fish which we are forbidden to eat are called in the Bible *unclean*, or not pure; and have been proved to be unhealthy. In the nineteenth chapter of Leviticus, the third book of the Pentateuch, we are again commanded to be a holy nation: ‘ And the Lord spoke unto Moses saying: “ Speak unto all the congregation of the children of Israel and say unto them: ‘ Ye shall be holy; for I the Lord your God am holy ’ ” ’ (verses 1, 2). In these verses we are given to understand that as a chosen people of

God we are duty-bound to do our utmost to follow in His ways, by dealing fairly and kindly with one another; by performing our actions in an honourable manner, and by causing our thoughts to be pure; as only in this way can we remain a holy nation. In order that this holiness should be kept at as high a pitch as possible, we are forbidden to eat such foods as have been termed as *unclean*. These dietary laws should teach us to master our inclinations, and that we must not permit ourselves to give way to our desires. We will now read what these laws permit or forbid us to eat.

We are permitted to eat the flesh of those animals which chew the cud and have cloven feet; but if the animal has only one of these signs, like the pig, which has cloven feet but does not chew the cud, it is forbidden. That part of the fat of an animal which was burnt during the sacrifices in the Temple is forbidden to us; but all other animal fat, and the fat of permitted birds, are permitted to be eaten. The flesh of an animal or bird that died from an illness or disease, or that was not killed according to the Jewish manner, is forbidden. Blood is very strictly forbidden, as we are told: 'And whatsoever man there be of the house of Israel, or of the strangers that sojourn among you, that eateth any manner of blood; I will even set my face against that soul that eateth blood, and will cut him off from among his people. For the life of the flesh is in the blood' (Leviticus, xvii, 10, 11). In order, therefore, to remove as much blood as possible, we soak the flesh in water for half an hour, and then salt it for one hour. We are forbidden to eat the part of the animal which is called the 'sinew of the hip which shrank' (גִּיד הַנָּשֶׁה) (because it reminds us of the sinew of the hip of Jacob which shrank when he wrestled with an angel). Those birds which are forbidden are called an abomination, or extremely hateful, and are mentioned in the eleventh chapter of Leviticus. Cruelty to animals or birds has always been regarded by Jews with the greatest horror, and is strictly forbidden in the Bible and by our Rabbis. To spare them any unnecessary pain we are forbidden to kill the parent with its young on the same day, or to cut off a piece of the flesh of a living creature, as was done by the people of many other nations at the time these laws were given; or to cause them pain when they are being slaughtered, and for this reason special laws were given laying down the most humane method of slaughter, which have received the praise of people qualified to judge in all nations. We are also forbidden to allow meat and milk to become mixed in any way; two sets of dishes are provided for this reason; one set for meat foods and the other for milk foods; and this law has been strictly observed by the Jewish people in every generation. After a meal at which meat foods have been partaken of, we must wait six hours before we are permitted to partake of milk foods. We are only permitted to eat fish which have both scales and fins. The eggs or milk of forbidden birds or animals, and the roe of forbidden fish, are all equally forbidden. All permitted food is known as ' Kosher ' (כָּשֵׁר); and all forbidden food is known as ' Trefah ' (טְרֵפָה).

We are forbidden to eat the fruit of a tree during the first three years after its planting, and such fruit is called ' Arlah ' (עָרְלָה).

We are forbidden to sow our fields or vineyards with a mixture of different kinds of seeds, and this is called ' Kilayim ' (כִּלְאַיִם). The wearing of a mixture of linen and wool is also strictly forbidden, as we are commanded: ' Neither shall a garment mingled of linen and woollen come upon thee' (Leviticus, xix, 19). Such a mixture is called ' Shatnes ' (שַׁעַטְנֵז).

## CHAPTER XVI

# SABBATH (שַׁבָּת)

The seventh day of the week is called a ' Holy Day of Rest ' (שַׁבַּת קֹדֶשׁ). After God had worked for six days, creating the world and all which it contains, He rested on the seventh. We must not think that He really needed to rest, as He is never tired; but He desired to impress upon us, by example, the great importance of resting on the seventh day.

During the ordinary week-days we are engaged in either mental or physical labours, and meet with frequent causes of worry and anxiety; consider, therefore, how very fortunate we are to possess a day on which we are commanded to put aside both our labours and our worries, and thus permit ourselves to become refreshed. We are not permitted, however, to pass the day in a lazy or useless manner, but we must bear in mind that besides being a day of rest, it is also a day of holiness. We should take advantage of it as a special weekly occasion upon which we are able to take stock at our leisure of our spiritual condition; to indulge in spiritual recreation; and to praise and sanctify God. We should utter prayers of thanks to our Heavenly Father for all His kindnesses towards us, permitting our thoughts to dwell on those kindnesses, and resolving to do our utmost to repay Him by obeying His will.

Some persons make it a habit on this day to visit those who are ill, and this is most certainly making good use of our Sabbath hours. We should not only visit those of our most intimate friends who are indisposed, but we should be prepared to ease the suffering even of those who are strangers to us, such as hospital patients. We should consider our own feelings if, God forbid, we were indisposed and had nothing to help us forget our pain, or the weariness of being bed-ridden; how delighted we should be if someone came to visit us and spent some time in cheering us up by their conversation. As God has blessed us with good health, we should therefore do our utmost to gladden the hours of those who are less fortunate.

The performance of many things which are permitted during the remainder of the week is forbidden on the Sabbath, because they would lead us in some manner to neglect the repose or desecrate the holiness of the day. We are not permitted to indulge in such strenuous games as football or cricket, or in any manner of recreation which requires exertion to the extent of fatiguing us.

We read in the Bible: ' It (the Sabbath) is a sign between Me and the children of Israel for ever, for in six days the Lord made the heaven and the earth and on the seventh day He rested and was refreshed' (Exodus, xxxi, 17). These words should teach us faithfully to observe this holy day as it is a sign of a covenant by which we became appointed as the chosen people of God.

We also read: 'And remember that thou wast a servant in the land of Egypt, and that the Lord thy God brought thee out from there with a mighty hand and by an outstretched arm; therefore the Lord thy God commanded thee to keep the Sabbath day' (Deuteronomy, v, 15); these words should teach us that the Sabbath must serve as a reminder of the Egyptian bondage, and that as God delivered us and granted us rest, so must we have consideration for our servants and animals and permit them to rest on this day.

The Sabbath is indeed a day of gladness and joy, and should be eagerly looked forward to. When we return from the House of God, after welcoming the Sabbath, we find that candles have been lit in order to make the room more festive and cheerful than usual, and that wine and two loaves of bread which are covered with a cloth stand upon the table. Wine is called by King David 'a joy and cheer', and it is therefore used on Sabbaths and Festivals as a symbol of the joy and cheer with which these days fill our homes; the two loaves of bread remind us of the double portion of Manna which was gathered on the sixth day in order to avoid the necessity of gathering any on the Sabbath; and the cloth which covers the bread reminds us of the dew which covered the Manna. The master of the house blesses his children, and with a cup of wine clasped in his hand, he commences to recite a prayer called 'Kiddush' (קִדּוּשׁ) which means 'sanctification'. This prayer consists of the first three verses of the second chapter of Genesis; a blessing over the wine, and a blessing in which we thank God for granting us the Sabbath and sanctifying us as His chosen people. When this cup of wine has been shared between all who are present, they all prepare themselves for the tasty dishes which have been specially prepared in honour of the Sabbath. After thanking God for providing us with food, each of our Sabbath meals is followed by songs of praise and cheerfulness which are called 'Zemiros' (זְמִירוֹת).

All the members of the family are united, perhaps for the first time since the previous Sabbath, and are filled with feelings of peace, contentment, and happiness. Worries and work are forgotten, and when we do remind ourselves of our ordinary week-day cares and anxieties, we appreciate how thankful we should be to our Father for granting us this day of rest and mental tranquillity.

A Kiddush prayer, which consists of a blessing over wine or spirits, is recited before commencing the Sabbath morning meal.

When this holy day has come to an end, a prayer is recited which is called 'Habdalah' (הַבְדָּלָה), meaning

' distinction '. This prayer consists of a blessing over wine; a blessing in which we thank God for creating light, as light was the first creation, and symbolises the light of the Torah with which we have dispelled the spiritual darkness of the nations; a blessing over spices, the aroma of which revives us from the feelings of sadness which are caused by the departure of this holy pleasurable day; and a blessing in which we thank God for the distinction which He has made between the Sabbath and other weekdays.

## CHAPTER XVII

# PASSOVER (פֶּסַח)

This is the first of the three chief festivals of the year, the other two being 'The Feast of Weeks' (שָׁבוּעוֹת) and 'The Feast of Tabernacles' (סֻכּוֹת). On each of these festivals our forefathers were commanded to journey to Jerusalem, even if they lived a far distance away, in order to come before God in the Temple with a gift offering of whatever they were able to afford.

### The Exodus from Egypt

The Sabbath before Passover is called 'The Great Sabbath' (שַׁבָּת הַגָּדוֹל), and the festival commences on the fifteenth day of the month Nisan. Its observance is meant to remind us how the Almighty God helped our forefathers to become free from the Egyptian slavery. Pharaoh, the Egyptian King, oppressed the Israelites (Jews have acquired this name because they are children of Jacob whose name was changed by God to Israel), who lived in his land, so that they suffered much hardship and were in continual fear. They cried for deliverance, and their Merciful Father broke their bonds by smiting Pharaoh and his land with plagues. After He had brought nine plagues upon them, and they still refused to permit the Israelites to become free, He told Moses that they were about to be smitten with a tenth plague, which would be the last, and through which all the first-born Egyptian children would die. Moses was therefore to command the Israelites to kill a lamb and sprinkle its blood upon their doorposts in order that the Angel, whom God would send to kill the Egyptians, would see the blood and *pass over* their houses. It is in remembrance of this event that we call the festival 'Passover'.

As a result of the tenth plague, Pharaoh became so greatly afraid of further punishment that he permitted the Israelites to leave Egypt as free men, and even did his utmost to hasten their departure. He did not grant them sufficient time to bake the dough which they had prepared, and they were therefore compelled to take it with them on their journey, and it was baked by the heat of the sun. In order to remind us of this sun-baked dough, God has commanded that during the days of the Passover festival we are not permitted to eat 'leavened bread' (חָמֵץ), but we must eat bread which has been specially prepared and which is called 'Unleavened Bread' (מַצָּה). We therefore also call this festival 'The Feast of Unleavened Bread' (חַג הַמַּצּוֹת).

We are unable even to imagine what freedom meant to those poor Hebrew slaves. We have the comforts of a home; the love and care of our parents; are able to do as we wish and go where we please; and are able to rest when we are tired. The Israelites in Egypt could not care for their children; and were filled with mental anguish at the thought that they would also become slaves, and be forced to suffer the agony which they were themselves undergoing. They were continually in dread of the taskmasters who watched over them and made them toil. These taskmasters delighted in finding fault with the work of the Israelites, or in complaining that they were lazy and did not work hard enough; they were then beaten unmercifully, and very often died under the lash. Consider, therefore, the joy and happiness with which they left their land of suffering, and with what heartfelt thanks they praised the Almighty Merciful God who had redeemed them. Because the Israelites were granted their freedom, we call this festival by yet a third name, 'The Season of our Freedom' (זְמַן חֵרוּתֵנוּ). The world appeared quite different to them from what it had ever been before, and such things as sunshine and the beauties of Nature which they had previously been unable fully to appreciate now became sources of wonder and pleasure to them. It seemed as if they had entered into a new life of which they knew very little, and instead of being a mere collection of slaves they now became united into one great nation; for this reason, Passover is sometimes called the 'Birthday of the Jewish Nation'.

The Egyptians worshipped idols and animals, and offered sacrifices to them; when, therefore, the

Israelites were delivered from slavery, they were also removed from this source of religious ignorance.

Our Rabbis have written: 'In every generation it is our duty to think that we ourselves went out from Egypt'. When we think of our forefathers in Egypt we must feel as if we ourselves are suffering with them; sharing their burdens; crying with them for the help of God, and rejoicing with them in their deliverance. To fulfil this duty is not as difficult as it may seem, as in every generation and in every land the Jewish people have been ill-treated and massacred; yet they have not given up hope, but like the Israelites of Egypt they cried unto God and He delivered them.

## Reminders of the Exodus

We are continually reminded of the going out from Egypt. We are reminded about it in the first of the Ten Commandments, in our morning and evening prayers, in the Kiddush; when we are commanded to keep the Sabbath; and in the portions of the Bible which are enclosed in the Tephillin. The reason for these continual reminders is to keep before us the mercy and power of God, and to teach us that He is at all times ready to help us, as He helped our forefathers. We should not delay to pray to Him, however, until we are in urgent need of His help, but we should daily offer words of thanks, praise and earnest appeal to Him, and He will then guard us from ever being in serious trouble of any description.

On the eve of the fourteenth day of Nisan a search is made for anything leavened which has been overlooked in our houses, as all leavened foods must be entirely removed before the festival begins. This searching is called 'The Searching for Leaven' (בְּדִיקַת חָמֵץ). After the first meal on the fourteenth day no more leavened food may be eaten, and that which remains, together with that which was gathered on the previous evening, is now burnt. This is called 'The Destruction of the Leaven' (בִּיעוּר חָמֵץ).

The fourteenth day of Nisan is called the 'Eve of Passover' (עֶרֶב פֶּסַח). On this day every first-born Jew is commanded to fast in remembrance that God saved the first-born of the Israelites when He slew those of the Egyptians. This fast is called 'The Fast of the First-born' (תַּעֲנִית בְּכוֹרִים). It is permissible, however, for them, after the morning service, to join with others in religious study, and then to partake of refreshments which have been provided for the occasion. Having in this way partaken of food, they become exempt from the necessity of fasting. When the eve of Passover occurs on Sabbath, the fast is observed on the preceding Thursday.

## CHAPTER XVIII

# PASSOVER (*continued*)

On each of the first two nights of Passover an important ceremony takes place in our homes which is called a 'Seder' (סֵדֶר), because during this ceremony a special order is followed, the word 'Seder' meaning 'order'. It is observed to impress upon us the miracles and wonders which God performed for our forefathers, and also to encourage us to discuss the events which are commemorated by the Passover festival. During the ceremony we read a book which is called an 'Haggadah' (הַגָּדָה), in which the mighty deliverance from Egypt is related at length, the word 'Haggadah' meaning 'relating'.

During the ceremony our tables are covered with the finest of cloths and our best dishes and cutlery are used. On the table before us are three cakes of unleavened bread (מַצּוֹת), and a dish upon which there are arranged some bitter herbs (מָרוֹר); vegetables (כַּרְפַּס); salt water; a mixture of nuts, apples and cinnamon which has been made into a paste by the addition of wine (חֲרוֹסֶת); a roasted bone (זְרוֹעַ), and a roasted egg (בֵּיצָה).

Two of the three מַצּוֹת represent the two loaves of bread which are used on Sabbaths and festivals as reminders of the double portion of Manna; the third מַצָּה should serve as a reminder of the 'bread of affliction' which our forefathers ate in Egypt.

The bitter herbs are to symbolise the bitterness which filled the lives of our forefathers during the time when they were in slavery.

The vegetables are dipped into salt water, as another symbol of slavery, and also to induce us to discuss their deliverance.

The חֲרוֹסֶת symbolises the mortar which our forefathers were forced to work into bricks; as it is sweet, it should remind us how God changed their lives from the bitterness of slavery to the sweetness of freedom, and should teach us that no matter how greatly we are troubled, we should pray to Him and trust in Him, and He will also help us as He helped our forefathers.

The roasted bone symbolises the special Passover offering of a lamb which was sacrificed in the Temple, and which was called 'The Offering of the Paschal Lamb' (קָרְבַּן פֶּסַח).

The roasted egg symbolises the festival offering which was sacrificed in the Temple on each of the three chief festivals, and which was called 'The Festival Offering' (קָרְבַּן חֲגִיגָה); the egg is also a symbol of mourning, and is present on the Seder table as a reminder of the beautiful Temple that has been destroyed, and that it is our duty to mourn its loss, and plead before God that it may speedily be rebuilt.

The Seder ceremony commences with the Sanctification (קִדּוּשׁ) over wine, and during the remainder of the ceremony three more cups of wine must be drunk. After reciting the Grace after Meals, when the third cup of wine is being filled, we also fill a separate cup in honour of Elijah, the Prophet. This reminds us of God's promise to bring us back to the land which He gave to our forefathers, and that this event will be preceded by the appearance of Elijah, who will prepare us for it.

The four middle days of Passover are called ' Weekday Festival ' (חוֹל הַמּוֹעֵד). God is aware that some people are unable to afford a holiday for eight days, and He therefore permits them to work during the four middle days. Those of us who work must remember, however, that although we are permitted to do what we find necessary, yet these days are still part of the festival, and we should, therefore, only perform such work as is absolutely essential and thus unavoidable.

The fourteenth day of the month Iyar (אִיָּר) was regarded as a festival day, and was called ' The Second Passover ' (פֶּסַח שֵׁנִי). It was observed by those who had been unable to celebrate the Passover festival on the appointed days, because they were on a journey or were defiled and therefore unable to participate in the Temple service.

CHAPTER XIX

# THE COUNTING OF THE OMER (סְפִירַת הָעוֹמֶר)

We are commanded in the Bible that on the second day of Passover we are to bring a measure, called an ' Omer ', of barley to the Temple and give it as an offering to God. We are then to count forty-nine days, and on the fiftieth day celebrate the ' Feast of Weeks '. When our forefathers lived in their own land, and possessed a Temple, they faithfully obeyed this commandment; but we, who possess neither a land nor a Temple, are unable to bring an offering before God, as offerings of any kind were only permitted to be offered in the Temple, which was situated in Jerusalem.

We are eager, however, to do our utmost to fulfil as much of this commandment as possible, and so we perform the counting of the days. After the evening service of each day, during the period between Passover and the Feast of Weeks, we recite the blessing: ' Blessed art Thou, O Lord our God, King of the Universe, who hast made us holy by Thy commandments, and hast commanded us concerning the counting of the Omer ', and the number of days which have passed are then mentioned. The counting of each day should lead us to consider our actions of that day, and decide if we have made sufficient use of the valuable gift of time. We should pray to our Heavenly Father for the forgiveness of our mistakes; that He should help us fully to understand the value of the days of life which He, in His great and everlasting mercy, grants to us, and that He should teach us how best to use them.

The days of the Omer are a very sad period as they remind us of the grievous troubles which in various ages have befallen our nation during the 'Omer' days. We have been murdered and robbed; Jewish books and Scrolls of the Law were publicly burned, and hundreds of Jews were put to death because of their loyalty to their religion. All manner of enjoyments are therefore forbidden during the six weeks before the Feast of Weeks, with the exception of the thirty-third day of the Omer, which is called in Hebrew לַ"ג בָּעוֹמֶר, because the letters ל"ג stand for the number thirty-three. Rabbi Akiba had a very large number of disciples, but a plague, or spreading disease, caused the death of many of them. On the thirty-third day of the Omer, however, the plague ceased, and so this day is called the 'Scholars' Feast'.

## CHAPTER XX

# THE FEAST OF WEEKS (חַג הַשָּׁבוּעוֹת)

This is the second of the three chief festivals, and is observed on the sixth and seventh days of the month Sivan. It is called by this name because it is observed just seven complete weeks from the second day of Passover.

In Palestine the summer commences much earlier than it does in more northern countries, and our forefathers had gathered in all their corn and wheat by the time that this festival had arrived; for this reason it is also called 'The Harvest Festival' (חַג הַקָּצִיר).

During this feast two loaves, which had been made from the first-fruits of the wheat harvest, were offered up in the Temple, and the Jews brought their first ripe fruits to be offered up there; for this reason we also call this festival the 'Day of the First-fruits' (יוֹם הַבִּכּוּרִים).

It must have been a beautiful sight to see the Jewish farmers flocking to the Temple to fulfil the command of offering their first-fruits. Those who had but a short distance to travel brought fresh fruit, figs and flowers; but those who had a long distance to travel brought dried fruits. They were filled with happiness, and sang ‘ O come let us go up to Zion, to the Lord our God’. When they came before the priest in the Temple they recited a prayer in which they related how God had delivered the Israelites from Egypt, and ended with the words: ‘ And now, behold, I have brought the first-fruits of the land which Thou, O Lord, hast given me.’ This prayer caused them to realise that although they had worked very hard at ploughing, sowing and reaping, yet their work had only proved successful because God had granted them His blessing. We, at the present time, cannot appear in the Temple and recite this prayer, but we should nevertheless realise that everything is granted to us by God, and that we are in duty bound to love, obey and honour Him for all His kindnesses towards us. In order to remind ourselves of God’s blessings to us, through nature, we decorate our synagogues with flowers and plants during these festival days.

This feast is also called ‘ The Season of the Giving of our Law’ (זְמַן מַתַּן תּוֹרָתֵנוּ), because it is the anniversary of the time when God gave the Ten Commandments to the Jewish people. By receiving this precious gift our forefathers became entirely free; as they had already gained their bodily freedom, now, through the Ten Commandments, they gained their spiritual freedom from the superstitions and idolatry of Egypt. Passover and the Feast of Weeks are therefore memorials of the redemptions of the Jewish People from bodily and spiritual slavery.

Our hearts should be filled with gratitude and love to God for choosing us from amongst all other nations to receive this great and holy gift; and as its possessors we are in duty bound to do our utmost to cause its teachings to become known to the other peoples of the world. We should also prove ourselves, both by word and action, to be examples to all with whom we come in contact; and be most careful that we should not bring shame or disrespect on the name of our nation. By causing ourselves to become worthy examples to others, we not only bring honour upon ourselves and our people, but we also honour and glorify the name of God; this is called 'Sanctification of God's name' (קִדּוּשׁ הַשֵּׁם). But if we cause ourselves, in any manner, to become bad examples to others, then we bring shame upon ourselves and our people; and derision upon the name of God, for choosing us as His Treasured People; this is called 'Profanation of God's Name' (חִלּוּל הַשֵּׁם).

In our daily prayers we rejoice that God has chosen us, and exclaim with great thanks in our hearts: 'Thou hast chosen us from all peoples and tongues, and hast brought us near unto Thy great name for ever in faithfulness, that we might in love give thanks unto Thee and declare Thy Unity. Blessed art Thou, O Lord, who hast chosen Thy people Israel in love.' The privilege that God has shown us is more clearly stated in the festival prayer: 'Thou hast chosen us from all peoples; Thou hast loved us and taken pleasure in us, and hast exalted us above all tongues;

Thou hast made us holy by Thy commandments, and brought us near unto Thy service, O our King, and hast called us by Thy great and holy name.'

We should always bear in mind the great responsibility which rests upon us as God's representatives, and should prove ourselves worthy of the honour which He has granted us.

The three days before the 'Feast of Weeks' are called 'The Three Days of Setting Bounds' (שְׁלֹשֶׁת יְמֵי הַגְבָּלָה) because Moses was commanded to set bounds round Mount Sinai before the giving of the Ten Commandments.

## CHAPTER XXI

# THE FOUR FASTS

THE Jewish people have not always been scattered amongst the nations of the world as they are at present, but, as we have already read, they possessed a city of their own, called Jerusalem, in which there was a Temple, or House of God. We must understand that God did not need a house in which to live, as 'the whole world is filled with His glory'; but because He loved the Jewish people so very much, He promised to be continually amongst them. A Temple was therefore built and all who were in trouble, or desired to offer a sacrifice or a prayer of thanks before God, would come to this Temple and pour out their hearts before the Merciful God, the Heavenly Father of all peoples. The Jews, however, did not realise their good fortune, and were continually disobeying the commandments of God. A prophet, called Jeremiah, warned them again and again to turn from their evil ways and observe God's commandments, and also warned them that if they continued to act against the will of God, then He would punish them by depriving them of their land and causing them to be made captives. But the warnings were disregarded, and God therefore punished them by allowing the Babylonians to defeat their armies. The Babylonians laid siege to Jerusalem, which was surrounded by very thick walls, on the tenth day of the month ‘ Teves ’, and the anniversary of this day is therefore observed as a public day of fasting, and is called ‘ The Fast of the Tenth Day of Teves ’ (צוֹם עֲשָׂרָה בְּטֵבֵת). The siege lasted almost two years, but at length, on the seventeenth day of the month Tammuz, under the leadership of their King, who was called Nebuchadnezzar, they broke through the walls. This day is therefore also observed as a public fast, and is called ‘The Fast of the Seventeenth Day of Tammuz’ (צוֹם שִׁבְעָה עָשָׂר בְּתַמּוּז). Fighting now took place in the city between the Jews and Babylonians. The Babylonians knew that if they could destroy the Temple the Jews would then lose heart and would be much more easily defeated; they therefore fought their way towards this holy building, and exactly three weeks after having broken through the city walls they achieved their purpose by destroying the Temple by fire. The Jews have possessed two Temples, and both of them were destroyed on the ninth day of the month Ab. Because these were the greatest tragedies that have ever happened to the Jewish people this day is regarded, next to the Day of Atonement, as the strictest and most important day of fasting, and the most mournful day in the Jewish year. This day of public fasting is called ‘ The Fast of the Ninth Day of Ab ’ (צוֹם תִּשְׁעָה בְּאָב). The three weeks between the fasts of Tammuz and Ab are observed as a period of sorrow, and on the Ninth Day of Ab the synagogue ark (אֲרוֹן הַקֹּדֶשׁ) is stripped of its curtain (פָּרוֹכֶת), and the 'Book of Lamentations', which was written by the Prophet Jeremiah, and special songs of mourning called קִינוֹת are chanted in a solemn tone. These lamentations and songs all describe the sufferings of our forefathers and the trouble and destruction that overtook Jerusalem.

We must not think that because thousands of years have passed since we were deprived of our land and our Temples we have at present no cause to mourn for those tragedies. We must remember that were it not for the sins of our forefathers, we should still have possessed both a land and a Temple, and should still have been a glorious nation; at present, however, we are scattered amongst the nations of the world, and are hated by the people of a great many of those nations; we are often made to suffer even death for faults which our enemies know we have not committed, but which they use as an excuse for attacking us.

Many persons are unable to understand why the Merciful God causes us to suffer for the sins of our forefathers, but such persons forget that the lessons which the capture of Jerusalem should have impressed upon us have been ignored, and that we cannot hope for the return of God's favour until, having realised that like our forefathers we are guilty of disobeying His will, we shall repent of our sins, and prove ourselves worthy of the honour of possessing a land of our own in which His glorious Divine Presence will again dwell. We must, therefore, return to God and His Torah, and deserve the fulfilment of His promise to turn these days of sorrow and fasting into days of rejoicing. Our God is indeed a Kind and Merciful Father, and He will listen to our prayers and observe our efforts to deserve His salvation.

The Sabbath before the fast of Ab is called 'The Sabbath of Vision' (שַׁבַּת חֲזוֹן) because on that day we read the first twenty-seven verses of the first chapter of the book of Isaiah, which begins with the words 'The vision of Isaiah, the son of Amoz, which he saw concerning Judah and Jerusalem', and contains words of warning and censure of the Israelites for neglecting to obey their God and His Torah.

The Sabbath after the fast of Ab is called 'The Sabbath of Comfort' (שַׁבַּת נַחֲמוּ), because on that day we read the first twenty-six verses of the fortieth chapter of the book of Isaiah, which begins with the words 'Comfort ye, comfort ye my people, saith your God', and contains words of comfort and hope.

This is indeed most wonderful, and contains an important lesson for us. The Jews had lost their land; their Temple had been burnt down, and they had themselves become captives, yet they did not lose their hope, and were comforted by the God against whom they had so grievously sinned. The true Jew, in every generation, does not permit his misfortunes to overcome him, but rather does his utmost to search out any ray of hope from which he can obtain fresh energy and encouragement. The Jewish nation has, times without number, been on the brink of coming to an end; enemies have surrounded it on all sides and the outlook was most threatening, yet the Jews put their hope and trust in the help of the Almighty God, and He did not forsake them. It was only when they repeatedly sinned against Him and would not repent, that He permitted them to be overcome; but even then He remained their Merciful Father, and comforted them with words of hope. Whenever, therefore, we find ourselves in a difficulty and cannot discover a solution, we should remember that there is One who is waiting for us to ask Him for His help, and who, if we trust in Him wholeheartedly, will most certainly show us a way of overcoming that difficulty.

As a result of the Babylonian victory the majority of the Jews were taken to Babylon as captives. Some Jews, however, were too weak to travel, or were forced to remain behind because of other reasons; and a man called Gedaliah was therefore appointed to govern over these people. He was a very good and kind man, but after ruling for but a few months he was cruelly murdered by a man who was of the royal blood and was desirous of being appointed King. Because he treated the Jews so kindly we annually observe the third day of the month Tishri (תִּשְׁרִי) as a public day of fasting, in memory of his murder, and it is therefore called ‘ The Fast of Gedaliah ’ (צוֹם גְּדַלְיָהוּ).

CHAPTER XXII

# THE NEW YEAR FESTIVAL (רֹאשׁ הַשָּׁנָה)

THIS festival commences on the first day of the month Tishri, and lasts for two days. It is a very important festival, as on these days God decides our fate during the forthcoming year. During the past year we have grievously sinned against Him, and it therefore becomes necessary for us to come before Him to plead for the forgiveness of our transgressions, and with a promise that we will do our utmost to avoid repeating them. We must think carefully of what we are saying and our utterances must be the expression of our deepest feelings, as nothing is hidden from the All-knowing God, and He knows how far our words are genuine. During the days of this festival God decides and, figuratively, writes down all that is to take place during the forthcoming year; for example, who shall live, and who shall die through illness, burning, drowning, accident, hunger, thirst, or in any other manner of death; who shall enjoy good health, and who shall suffer bad health; who shall be happy, and who shall be unhappy; who shall earn sufficient for their needs, and who shall be in want; these and many other things are decided. We should therefore realise the tremendous danger with which we are faced, lest God will decide against us and the great necessity of pleading before Him with all our hearts and minds that He, in His abounding kindness and mercy, should not decide to inflict upon us the penalty which we deserve, but should grant us another year of life and good health in order that we should be able to correct our faults and obey His commandments. The great just God, who judges the world, is also a kind and merciful Father, and is ever ready to forgive all who come before Him, if only they are truly repentant and mean to do better.

Because we are judged during this festival, it is also called 'The Day of Judgment' (יוֹם הַדִּין); and because all our deeds of the past year are remembered by God during this festival, it is also called 'The Day of Remembrance' (יוֹם הַזִּכָּרוֹן).

Before we commence our pleadings for forgiveness before the throne of our Heavenly King we must forgive all those who have sinned against us, and seek the forgiveness of those against whom we have sinned; as until we have forgiven one another we cannot expect God's forgiveness.

During this festival the synagogue ark has a white curtain, and many people are clothed in white garments, as a reminder of the great necessity of purifying ourselves before God through charity, prayers and repentance. The ram's horn (שׁוֹפָר) is blown on this festival, serving as an additional reminder of the urgency of making our peace with God; and also, as a request to Him to forgive our transgressions for the sake of Abraham, our father; as Abraham was the first to discover and worship the True Living Everlasting God, and we are his children, or descendants. If your father had a very great friend, and you in some manner offended him and he was about to punish you, you would plead with him, that because of the great friendship which he shared with your father, he should overlook your offence. In a like manner we plead with the Almighty Merciful God that although we have sinned against Him, yet He should forgive us for the sake of Abraham who was His obedient servant and true friend, and was ready to sacrifice his only son, Isaac, for whom he had waited so long, because God had commanded him to do so.

When Abraham was stopped, by a heavenly voice, from sacrificing his son, he was told to sacrifice, in his stead, a ram which was near by; and it is as a reminder of this very important event that the horn of a ram is used. Because the horn is blown during these new year days, we also call this festival ‘ A Day of Sounding the Horn ’ (יוֹם תְּרוּעָה).

After the ‘ Kiddush ’ (קִדּוּשׁ) prayer, we partake of some sweet fruit which has been dipped in honey, after having said a blessing and a prayer in which we ask God for a good and prosperous year. On the afternoon of the first day of this festival (or of the second day, if the first day was on Sabbath) we assemble near a running stream, and recite the verses: 'Who is a God like unto Thee, that pardoneth iniquity, and passeth by the transgression of the remnant of His heritage? He retaineth not His anger for ever, because He delighteth in Mercy. He will turn again and have compassion upon us; He will subdue our iniquities; and Thou wilt cast all their sins into the depths of the sea. Thou wilt show faithfulness to Jacob, and loving kindness to Abraham, as Thou hast sworn unto our fathers from the days of old' (Micah, vii, 18-20). Other verses and prayers are also recited. This ceremony is called 'Tashlich' (תַּשְׁלִיךְ), which means 'Thou wilt cast', because the purpose of the assembling of Jews is to *cast away* their sins.

A valuable feature of this festival is that it provides us with an opportunity of noting our failings of the past year, which should cause us to resolve that, in the coming year, we will do our utmost to improve upon them, and become true and faithful children of our Heavenly Merciful Father.

## CHAPTER XXIII

# THE DAYS OF REPENTANCE

THE first ten days of the month Tishri are called 'The Ten Days of Repentance' (עֲשֶׂרֶת יְמֵי תְשׁוּבָה), or 'Solemn Days' (יָמִים נוֹרָאִים).

We have read that the New Year festival is observed on the first two of these days, and that during those days God judges the world, and decides the happenings of the forthcoming year.

Our Merciful Heavenly Judge, however, is not eager to punish us and cause us to be ill or unhappy; and so He eagerly awaits our repentance and prayers. Some persons are extremely good, whilst others are extremely bad, but most persons are neither of one class nor the other. God, therefore, does not hurriedly come to a final decision regarding the manner of year which He should grant us, but allows us another eight days, during which He observes our efforts at self-improvement. That He will deal mercifully with us if we turn from our sinful ways is taught in the verse: 'Let the wicked forsake his way, and the unrighteous man his thoughts; and let him return unto the Lord, and He will have mercy upon him; and to our God, for He will abundantly pardon' (Isaiah, lv, 7).

What is meant by repentance? When a person repents with all his heart and mind he realises how grievously he has sinned against God, the great and faithful Father, who has fed and supported him and done so much for his benefit; and he therefore turns from his evil ways and returns to the path of life willed by God. It is this 'returning to God' that is the essence of repentance. He appears before God, giving expression to his earnest regret for past misdeeds and promising that henceforth he will do his utmost to obey God's commandments. He also pleads that as he is merely human and liable to sin, he desires the guardianship of God, and that He should send him His help to fight against the temptation of doing wrong. If God knows that our words are sincere, and that we earnestly intend to fulfil our promises, then He forgives us, and grants us another year of life, good health and happiness.

Because these days are called Days of Repentance, we are not to think that they are the only days upon which we are to come before God with a contrite spirit; it is a daily duty to repent for the sins which have been committed each day. Some persons do not care how they behave all through the year, as they make up their minds that they will repent during these days and will thus gain God's forgiveness. Such persons forget that the All-knowing God is aware of their thoughts and intentions; and when they come before Him and repent of their misdeeds, He will not accept their repentance. Although He desires us to feel heartfelt regret for our sins, yet He prefers us to do our utmost to guard against the committing of sins. It is impossible to go through life without committing a sin, but we must not permit this to become an excuse for wrongdoing. We must do all that is in our power to cast from us the temptation to commit an action which is displeasing before God, even if we imagine that such an action would benefit us.

The Sabbath which occurs during these days is called 'The Sabbath of Repentance' (שַׁבַּת שׁוּבָה), because the first word of the verses from the book of Hosea which are read on this day is 'Return' (שׁוּבָה), and bids us to return with contrition to our Heavenly Father.

CHAPTER XXIV

# THE DAY OF ATONEMENT (יוֹם הַכִּפּוּר)

The tenth day of the month Tishri is called the 'Day of Atonement', and is entirely spent in prayers of supplication before the Heavenly Judge, our Merciful Father, to accept our contrition and cleanse us from our sins; and for this reason it is the holiest day of the year.

We are commanded in the Bible: 'And this shall be a statute for ever unto you; that in the seventh month, on the tenth day of the month, ye shall afflict yourselves' (Leviticus, xvi, 29), and we therefore observe a strict period of fasting from the eve following on the ninth day of Tishri until the eve following on the tenth day, as we are also commanded, 'And it shall be unto you a Sabbath of rest, and ye shall afflict yourselves in the ninth day of the month, at even; from even unto even shall ye celebrate your Sabbath' (Leviticus, xxiii, 32).

During the New Year Festival God decides and figuratively *writes* down the kind of year which we shall have, and then allows us a further eight days during which He observes our efforts of improvement. On the last of these days, the Day of Atonement, He reconsiders His previous decision and is influenced by our behaviour during those days; and to whatever He now decides He figuratively puts His *seal*. On this day, therefore, we are given another opportunity to humble ourselves before the throne of God, and throw ourselves entirely on His mercy. When a child has disobeyed, or in any manner offended its parents, it will feel very unhappy until it has sought and obtained their pardon; in a like manner we must beseech the Heavenly Merciful Judge, who is always our loving Father, to pardon our acts of disobedience against Him. It is the heart and mind that God desires of us, and we are far more certain of obtaining His forgiveness by uttering merely a few words of heartfelt prayer than by reciting a multitude of prayers which are mere lip-service.

Some persons plead for forgiveness and promise to forsake their evil ways, but they have no intention of fulfilling their promise; such persons wilfully offend God, and will be severely punished.

We have already dealt with the great need for repentance and prayer, but we are also taught the necessity of Charity for the purpose of obtaining forgiveness. The need for charity is very frequently mentioned in our prayers, and is taught in the fifty-eighth chapter of the book of Isaiah, which is read during the morning service of the Day of Atonement, as it is written: 'Is not this the fast which I have chosen? to loose the bonds of wickedness, to undo the bands of the yoke, and to let the oppressed go free, and that thou break every yoke? Is it not to deal thy bread to the hungry, and that thou bring the poor that are cast out to thy house? When thou seest the naked, that thou cover him; and that thou hide not thyself from thine own flesh' (Verses 6, 7).

We must remember that we are all children of one Father, and that it is our duty to show mercy and kindness to one another, before we can expect God to guard us and judge us with mercy and kindness.

The most solemn and important portion of this great day is its closing hours. The whole day is spent in prayer and supplication before God, and we have repeatedly confessed our sins, and pleaded: 'Our Father, our King, *write* us in the book of life.' He has hearkened unto our prayers and pleadings, and during the last hours of the day He decides our fate, and figuratively *seals* his decision. During the last service, therefore, we do not say '*write* us', but '*seal* us in the book of life'. This service is called 'Neilah' (נְעִילָה), which means 'closing', and should therefore impress upon us that very little time remains in which to seek our peace with God, as the day is drawing to an end, and the gates of heaven will soon be *closed* to us.

We are indeed most fortunate to possess such a day during which we are able to purify ourselves from the sins which we have committed, and which remove us further and further from our pure, holy, eternal God. We are also extremely fortunate in possessing as our judge such a Merciful God who is eager to pardon and is full of sympathy and kindness towards all His children, and especially towards those who do their utmost to honour and obey Him.

Those persons who have neglected to seek forgiveness from their neighbours, and themselves granted forgiveness, *must* do so before this holy day commences, as this is one of the chief conditions upon which we can hope for God's forgiveness.

CHAPTER XXV

# THE FEAST OF TABERNACLES (חַג הַסֻּכּוֹת)

THIS festival commences on the fifteenth day of the month Tishri and lasts for seven days, but as it is immediately followed by another festival which lasts for two days, it is regarded by some persons as lasting for nine days. It is observed as a reminder of the care and protection which God granted our forefathers during their forty years' journey from Egypt to Canaan; and also, to remind us that they had, during this journey, to live in booths or tabernacles (סֻכּוֹת). They were continually moving from one place to another, and it was therefore impossible for them to provide themselves with houses of brick or stone, and they were compelled to manage with booths which could easily be set up and taken down. In order that we should be reminded of this, we are commanded to build ourselves booths and live in them during these festival days, and for this reason it is called the 'Feast of Tabernacles'. During these days we are to eat and live entirely in booths, unless the weather is very cold or wet, so that it would be risky to dispose ourselves to it; under such circumstances we are permitted to live in our houses, but we must return to spend as much time in the booths as possible. We are not told very much regarding the manner in which we are to build the booths, except that the most important part of the building is the roof. We are not permitted to make a solid roof, as that would render it a permanent dwelling, but we must make it of branches, or leaves, or certain other things, which are to be put on neither too loosely nor too thickly, but just loosely enough to allow us to see the stars through it. We must decorate the booth and make it as comfortable as possible.

When we leave our stone or brick-built house, with all its security and comfort, and live in this frail booth which is but a slight protection against wind and rain, we are reminded that our forefathers were compelled to live in such frail buildings, and had to depend on the mercy of the Almighty God to protect them from the cold winds, rain and other dangers; and that He provided them with meat, food, water, and all their necessities. This should cause us to consider how very much we are also dependent on His everlasting mercy and kindness, and that although our homes afford us more protection than our forefathers obtained from their booths, yet, unless we have His care and guardianship, we are far less secure than they were. In the booth we are not surrounded by all our possessions, and we are therefore reminded that those possessions are only ours because God has blessed us and granted them to us; and that unless He continues to grant us our requirements as He did our forefathers, then our possessions are of little value, and we are in far greater need than they were.

This festival is also called the ‘ Feast of Ingathering ’ (חַג הָאָסִיף), because our forefathers, by the time that this festival arrived, had gathered in all the produce of their fields. As on the Feast of Weeks, they offered heartfelt thanks to God for blessing their work, and realised that notwithstanding their hard work at tilling, sowing and attending to the ground in many other ways, yet without God's assistance that work would have been in vain. Some of the fruit which they had grown was hung in the booth, and had the double effect of beautifying it, and also of serving as a continual reminder of God's blessings and help.

We are commanded in the Bible: ‘ And ye shall take unto you on the first day the fruit of goodly-trees, branches of Palm-trees and boughs of thick trees and willows of the brook; and ye shall rejoice before the Lord your God seven days ’ (Leviticus, xxiii, 40). In order to obey this command we take in our hands four kinds of plants (אַרְבָּעָה מִינִים), a citron (אֶתְרוֹג), a branch of a palm-tree (לוּלָב), branches of myrtle (הֲדַסִּים), and branches of willow (עֲרָבוֹת). The branches of myrtle and willow are tied to the bottom of the palm-branch, and are held in the right hand, while the citron is held in the left hand; a blessing is then made, and the plants are waved in all directions, as an acknowledgment that the whole world is filled with the power and glory of the Almighty God. During the recital of the psalms of praise, called ‘ Hallel ’ (הַלֵּל), the plants are also waved in all directions for the same reason.

Our Rabbis have taught us that each of these plants has a message for us. The citron is shaped like the human heart and is used in the service of God, so must we cause our thanks and praise before God to flow from the depths of our hearts; the palm-branch stands upright, but bends when it is shaken in acknowledgment of the power and glory of God; so must we, who usually stand upright, bend in gratefulness before Him (at certain places in our prayers); the leaves of myrtle resemble the human eye and are always turned upwards, so should we cause our eyes to be upturned to God in hope and faith; the leaves of the willow resemble the human lips, and are used in the service of the Almighty God, so must we guard our lips that they should continually be used for the uttering of good and holy words, and for comforting those who are in trouble or despair.

The period from the third to the eighth day is observed as 'Weekday Festival' (חול הַמּוֹעֵד), the meaning of which has been explained in chapter xviii.

CHAPTER XXVI

## THE FEAST OF TABERNACLES (*continued*)

THIS festival is also called in our prayers the 'Season of our Rejoicing' (זְמַן שִׂמְחָתֵנוּ), as we are particularly commanded in the Bible to rejoice during these days: 'And thou shalt rejoice in thy feast, thou, and thy son, and thy daughter, and thy manservant, and thy maidservant, and the Levite, and the stranger, and the fatherless, and the widow, that are within thy gates' (Deuteronomy, xvi, 14). These words should teach us that it is not only necessary for us to rejoice, but that we must do our utmost also to cause pleasure and rejoicing to those who are less fortunate than ourselves.

The seventh day of this festival is called the 'Great Hoshanna' (הוֹשַׁעְנָה רַבָּא). During each of the previous six days, except on Sabbath, we go round the synagogue, holding the four plants in our hands, and chanting a prayer, each verse of which commences with the word 'Hoshanna' (הוֹשַׁע נָא). On the seventh day we go around the synagogue seven times, chanting prayers, each verse of which commences with the word 'Hoshanna', and this day is therefore called 'The Great Hoshanna'. This day is also regarded as the last upon which we can hope for a favourable decree. After having written and sealed His decision regarding the kind of year He will grant us, God on this day gives His verdict, which is unalterable.

The eighth and ninth days are together called 'The Eighth Day of Solemn Assembly' (שְׁמִינִי עֲצֶרֶת). On the first of these days we eat our meals in the booth, or tabernacle, for the last time, and it is therefore regarded as a final, or closing, day of the festival. During the morning service we pray that God should grant us wind and rain in their due season.

The second of these days is also named 'The Rejoicing of the Law' (שִׂמְחַת תּוֹרָה). On each Sabbath during the year a portion (סִדְרָא) of the Torah, or five books of Moses, is read; and the reading finishes and immediately recommences on this day. The teachings of the Torah should be ever in our minds, and it is therefore necessary that we should continually be reminded of them; it is for this reason that the reading of the Torah must never cease. The sacred Scrolls of the Law (סִפְרֵי תוֹרָה) are carried in procession around the synagogue, and songs of praise are chanted. In these songs we express joy and gratitude to our Heavenly Father, who has appointed us His chosen people by honouring us with such a treasure, and has permitted us to live to hear the reading of the Torah completed and recommenced. This day should teach us, however, that it is not sufficient for us merely to rejoice with the Torah, but that we must also find pleasure in fulfilling the laws and commandments which it contains; we must remember that it was given into our charge, and that we are therefore in duty bound to cause its greatness and holiness to become recognised amongst the nations of the world. Our forefathers were often called upon to make great sacrifices in defence of the Torah, but they were ever ready to defend it even with their lives; we shall also meet with occasions when our love for the Torah will be challenged, and we should therefore remember the words of our daily prayers: 'Therefore, O Lord our God, when we lie down and when we rise up we will meditate on Thy statutes; yea, we will rejoice in the words of Thy Law and in Thy commandments for ever; for they are our life and the length of our days, and we will meditate on them day and night.' Right through the ages it was the Torah which preserved us, and which in turn we have done our utmost to preserve. In our Sabbath prayers we sing: 'It (the Torah) is a tree of life to them that grasp it, and of them that uphold it every-one is rendered happy. Its ways are ways of pleasantness and all its paths are peace.'

It is regarded as a special honour to be called, during the morning service of this day, to the reading of the last portion of the Torah, and he who is so honoured is called 'Bridegroom of the Law' (חֲתַן תּוֹרָה); it is also regarded as a special honour to be called to the reading of the first portion of the Torah, and he who is so honoured is called ‘ Bridegroom of the Beginning ’ (חֲתַן בְּרֵאשִׁית).

CHAPTER XXVII

## FEAST OF DEDICATION (חֲנוּכָּה)

THIS feast commences on the twenty-fifth day of the month Kislev, and continues for eight days. It is observed as a minor festival, or a festival during which we are permitted to work, and celebrates the victory of the Maccabean heroes over the Syrian army. The King of Syria had conquered Judea, and was determined to destroy the Jewish religion and therefore the Jewish nation, as without their religion Jews would be unable to continue as a separate nation, and would be swallowed up amongst the other peoples of the world. With this purpose in view he sent messengers to erect idols in different parts of the land, and to force the Jews to worship them. Resistance appeared to be hopeless, and it seemed as if the end of Judaism had come; but the Almighty God did not permit such a tragedy to occur.

A Jew, afraid of angering the King, was about to bow before the idol which had been erected in Modin, a village in Judea; but Mattathias, who was a true priest and wholehearted servant of the Living Everlasting God, became filled with righteous anger against him, and struck him a death-blow. This act encouraged the people, and they attacked and killed the King's messengers, with the result that they were called upon to defend themselves against the Syrians who fought to avenge the murders. The Jews were led by Mattathias's second son, Judas, who called himself 'Judas Maccabeus' because they had as their motto the words מִי־כָמֹכָה בָּאֵלִם יְהוָֹה (Who is like unto Thee, among the gods, O Lord?), and the first letters of these words form together the word מַכַּבִּי (Maccabee). Judas and his men fought bravely for three years, and finally defeated their enemies and drove them out of the land. Their first action after this victory was to purify the Temple, as the Syrians had set up idols there and offered sacrifices of unclean animals upon the holy altars; and in remembrance of this renewal of the holiness of the Temple, of new vessels being brought and altars built, we call this feast the 'Feast of Dedication'.

In the Temple there was a lamp which was called נֵר תָּמִיד (Continual Light), because God had commanded that it must never be permitted to become extinguished. For this lamp specially prepared oil was needed, which took eight days to prepare, and became impure if handled by a non-Jew. The Synagogue, the present House of God, takes the place of the Temple which has been destroyed, and we therefore have a נֵר תָּמִיד burning near the holy ark (אֲרוֹן הַקֹּדֶשׁ). When Judas desired to rekindle the lamp he only possessed one jar of pure oil, as the remaining jars had been opened and the oil defiled by the Syrians. This oil was only sufficient to burn for one day, but on the twenty-fifth day of Kislev, Judas rekindled the lamp, and put his trust in God to cause it to continue to burn until fresh oil could be prepared. The Almighty Merciful God never fails us if we put our sincere trust in Him, and so He performed a miracle by causing the oil to burn for eight days. As a reminder of this miracle we also call this feast ‘The Feast of Lights’; and from the twenty-fifth day of Kislev we kindle lights on each of the following eight evenings. On the first evening we kindle one light towards the right, and continue to add an extra light towards the left on each evening, until, on the eighth evening, we have eight lights. The light which has been added is always kindled first, and this is preceded by two blessings in which we thank God for commanding us concerning the kindling of the lights, and also refer to the miracles performed by God on behalf of the Jewish people; on the first night, a third blessing is added in which we thank God for granting us life again to reach this festival. We are not permitted to make any profane use of these lights, and it is customary not to do any manner of work during the time they are burning. A hymn is chanted, which is called מָעוֹז צוּר because it commences with those words.

During the days of this feast the Hallel (הַלֵּל) is recited, and special prayers are said (עַל הַנִּסִּים וּבִימֵי מַתִּתְיָהוּ) which relate of the Jewish deliverance from the hands of the Syrians.

The Maccabean heroes fought for Judaism in one of its times of greatest need, and proved to the other peoples of the world that God is always ready to assist those who try to defend that which is right and just. These heroes had a deep-rooted love for their religion, and were therefore ready to defend it even at the cost of their lives. We should consider, therefore, how earnestly, and with what zest, we, who are at liberty to practise our religion, should fulfil its demands; and how great is the duty upon us to prove ourselves worthy of the honour which is bestowed upon us, as Jews and descendants of those Maccabean heroes.

## CHAPTER XXVIII

# FEAST OF PURIM (פּוּרִים)

THIS feast is observed on the fourteenth day of the month Adar, and, like the 'Feast of Dedication', is a minor festival; it is observed in remembrance of an occasion when the Jews were in grave danger, and the Almighty Merciful God answered their prayers and granted them salvation.

Ahasuerus, King of Persia, married a Jewish maiden called Esther, who had been brought up from birth by her cousin, Mordecai. This king commanded his subjects to bow before Haman, his chief minister; but Mordecai refused to obey this command, as Jews should only bow before the glory and greatness of God. This caused Haman to become very angry, and he decided that as Mordecai was a member of the Jewish nation he would punish all the Jews in the kingdom. He therefore persuaded the King to decree their extermination, and cast lots to determine the month and day on which he should carry out his evil plan; the Hebrew word for 'lots' is 'Purim' (פּוּרִים). According to the result of the lots, the thirteenth day of the month Adar was appointed as the day of slaughter, and Haman was very glad, as he knew that Moses died during the month Adar and forgetting that Moses was also born in this month, thought that it was a sign of ill-omen for the Jewish people. He sent messengers to all parts of the kingdom to inform the people that they were permitted to attack and slay their Jewish neighbours on the appointed day, and help themselves to their property. The Jews were exceedingly alarmed when they heard of the impending danger, and Mordecai sent to Esther requesting her to plead before the King on behalf of her people. She was afraid to go before the King, as it was a Persian custom that anyone who came before him uninvited would be put to death unless he held out a golden sceptre towards him. Mordecai, however, persuaded her to risk even her life in an effort to save the Jews, and she requested them to join with her in fasting for three days and in pleading before God to grant her success. 'And if I perish, I perish', she bravely declared. When she came before the King she was delivered from death, and eventually appealed to him to save her people from the grave and fearful doom which Haman had plotted against them. The King, who did not remember giving Haman this permission to have the Jews slain, became very angry, and as Haman had ordered a gallows to be erected upon which to hang Mordecai, the King ordered that Haman and his ten sons should be hanged upon it. He now promoted Mordecai to the post of chief minister, which had previously been held by Haman, and he thus obtained the power to send messengers throughout the kingdom to inform the people that the permission to attack the Jews had been withdrawn, and that the Jews were permitted to defend themselves against their attackers.

We fast on the thirteenth day of the month Adar, in remembrance of the fast which was ordered by Esther, and this day is therefore called 'The Fast of Esther' (תַּעֲנִית אֶסְתֵּר). The fourteenth day of Adar is observed as a day of rejoicing and thankfulness to the Almighty Merciful God for His great deliverance. During the night and morning services the 'Book of Esther' (מְגִלָּה) is read and special prayers are said (עַל הַנִּסִּים וּבִימֵי מָרְדְּכַי) which relate the Jewish deliverance from the hand of Haman. The fifteenth day of Adar is also observed as a day of rejoicing, in remembrance of the Jews who lived in Shushan, which was the capital of Persia; they continued to defend themselves on the fourteenth day and observed the feast on the fifteenth day, which is therefore called 'Purim of Shushan' (שׁוּשַׁן פּוּרִים).

The 'Feast of Purim' should teach us that even when we are in a land where we deem ourselves perfectly secure from troubles we should not put our trust in mankind but in the Almighty Guardian, the Faithful Rock of Salvation. We should learn from Mordecai who, even after being appointed to the post of chief minister to a king who reigned over one hundred and twenty-seven provinces, remained a true servant to God, and did his utmost for the welfare of his people. We should also learn from Esther, who was prepared to endanger her life for the lives of her people, the spirit of self-sacrifice which is so strikingly contained in her words: 'And if I perish, I perish.' They have taught us that occasions arise when a whole nation can be saved by the action and courage of a single person, and we should therefore be ever ready to grasp our opportunities and make the utmost use of them.

On Purim we must send presents to one another (מִשְׁלוֹחַ מָנוֹת), and provide the needy with means for enjoying themselves.

## CHAPTER XXIX

# GOD AND HIS TORAH

WE HAVE read in this book of the more important Laws and Commandments of our religion; we have had their reasons explained, have learnt how very important it is for us, and for the welfare of our nation, that we should obey them. There are some persons, however, who neglect to obey some of these Laws of the Torah, because they rely upon their own wisdom to decide which of them they should observe and which they should neglect. Such persons forget that *all* the laws and commandments of the Torah were commanded by the All-wise God; and that it is, therefore, very wrong of them to dare to compare their wisdom with the wisdom of God, by observing only that with which their own understanding or reasoning agree.

Other persons, as we have read in a previous chapter, neglect to observe the Torah because it interferes with their convenience or pleasures; the Dietary laws are neglected because they force them to practise an irksome self-control; the observance of Sabbaths and Festivals is neglected for the sake of monetary gain, or because they, in some manner, interfere with their pleasures; and so they continue to find ridiculous reasons with which to excuse their neglect of God's will.

We must guard ourselves from ever being guilty of such foolish, and very sinful, conduct; and must remember that the teachings of the Torah are the very life of our religion, and are therefore vitally important for the continued existence of the Jewish nation. We must approach the Torah and its teachings with a spirit of inquiry, meditation and docility, and not with a spirit of ridicule; it must be regarded as a treasured gift, given from God for our guidance and instruction; its contents must be recognised as a basis and rule of life, making known to us our duty towards God and our fellow-beings; and we should be prepared to sacrifice our greatest or dearest pleasures, if they are in conflict with its teachings. If or when we are faced with the temptation to disobey these teachings, we should realise that by obeying our selfish inclinations we are seriously offending against the honour of God, who has given us laws and commandments for our own welfare. As a safeguard against any such temptation we should continually keep in mind the overwhelming debt of gratitude which we owe to God, who is our Merciful Heavenly Father and Guardian. We should be ever ready to give expression to these feelings of gratitude, and should wholeheartedly exclaim those words of blessing and glorious praise which are part of our daily morning prayers: 'Blessed be the Lord for evermore. Amen and Amen. Blessed be the Lord out of Zion, Who dwelleth in Jerusalem. Praise ye the Lord. Blessed be the Lord God, the God of Israel, Who alone doeth wondrous things; and blessed be His glorious name for ever; and let the whole earth be filled with His glory. Amen and Amen.

'Blessed art Thou, O Lord, the God of Israel our father, from everlasting to everlasting. Thine, O Lord, is the greatness, and the power, and the glory, and the victory, and the majesty: for all that is in the heaven and in the earth is Thine; Thine, O Lord, is the kingdom, and the supremacy as head over all. Riches and honour come of Thee, and Thou rulest over all; and in Thine hand are might and power; and in Thine hand it is to make great, and to give strength unto all. Now, therefore, our God, we give thanks unto Thee, and praise Thy glorious name.'

## APPENDIX

# THE JEWISH CALENDAR

### Nisan

נִיסָן (Nisan). The Sabbath before Passover is called שַׁבָּת הַגָּדוֹל (The Great Sabbath).

*14th:* עֶרֶב פֶּסַח (Eve of Passover). Fast of First-born.

*15th to 22nd:* פֶּסַח (Passover).

*16th:* סְפִירַת הָעוֹמֶר (Commencement of the counting of the Omer).

### Iyar

אִיָּר (Iyar). *4th:* פֶּסַח שֵׁנִי (Second Passover).

*18th:* לַ״ג בָּעוֹמֶר (Thirty-third day of the Omer).

### Sivan

סִיוָן (Sivan). *3rd to 6th:* שְׁלֹשֶׁת יְמֵי הַגְבָּלָה (The Three Days of Setting Bounds).

*6th and 7th:* שָׁבוּעוֹת (Feast of Weeks).

### Tammuz

תַּמּוּז (Tammuz). *17th:* צוֹם שִׁבְעָה עָשָׂר בְּתַמּוּז (Fast of the Seventeenth day of Tammuz).

### Ab

אָב (Ab). The first Sabbath is called שַׁבַּת חֲזוֹן (Sabbath of Vision).

*9th:* צוֹם תִּשְׁעָה בְּאָב (Fast of the ninth day of Ab). The Second Sabbath is called שַׁבַּת נַחֲמוּ (Sabbath of Comfort).

*15th:* חֲמִשָּׁה עָשָׂר בְּאָב (Fifteenth day of Ab) (observed as a minor festival because, on this day, the tribe of Benjamin became reconciled with the Israelites).

### Ellul

אֱלוּל (Ellul). The ram's horn (שׁוֹפָר) is blown each morning, during this month, except on Sabbath, to remind us of the solemn time which is approaching. Prayers of atonement (סְלִיחוֹת) are said each day from the last Sunday in the month until רֹאשׁ הַשָּׁנָה.

### Tishri

תִּשְׁרִי (Tishri). *1st and 2nd:* רֹאשׁ הַשָּׁנָה (New Year Festival).

*3rd:* צוֹם גְּדַלְיָהוּ (Fast of Gedaliah).

First ten days are called עֲשֶׂרֶת יְמֵי תְשׁוּבָה (The Ten Days of Repentance). The Sabbath which occurs during these days is called שַׁבַּת שׁוּבָה (Sabbath of Repentance).

*10th:* יוֹם כִּפּוּר (Day of Atonement).

*15th to 21st:* סֻכּוֹת (Feast of Tabernacles).

*21st:* הוֹשַׁעְנָא רַבָּא (The Great Hashanna).

*22nd and 23rd:* שְׁמִינִי עֲצֶרֶת (Eighth Day of Solemn Assembly).

*23rd:* Also called שִׂמְחַת תּוֹרָה (Rejoicing of the Law).

CHESHVAN OR MARCHESHVAN

חֶשְׁוָן or מַרְחֶשְׁוָן (Cheshvan or Marcheshvan). The minor fasts of Monday, Thursday and Monday (שֵׁנִי חֲמִישִׁי וְשֵׁנִי) are observed at the end of this month.

KISLEV

כִּסְלֵיו (Kislev). *25th* (lasting for eight days): חֲנוּכָּה (Feast of Dedication).

TEVES

טבת (Teves). *10th:* צוֹם עֲשָׂרָה בְּטֵבֵת (The Fast of the Tenth Day of Teves).

## Shevat

שְׁבָט (Shevat). *15th:* חֲמִשָּׁה עָשָׂר בִּשְׁבָט. This day is the New Year for Trees. On the last Sabbath in this month, or on the first day of the next month if it falls on a Sabbath, we read, in addition to the weekly portion of the Law, a special portion (Exodus, xxx, 11-16), in which the Israelites were forbidden to count themselves, but each person over the age of twenty years was annually to give a half-shekel; these were then counted, and were spent on the requirements of the Tabernacle. This special portion is called פָּרָשַׁת שְׁקָלִים (The Portion of the Shekels). We make a collection in our synagogues on the first night of פּוּרִים, and as we have no Tabernacle or Temple to care for, we give the money to the poor.

## Adar

אֲדָר (Adar). On the Sabbath before פּוּרִים we read, in addition to the weekly portion of the Law, a special portion (Deuteronomy, xxv, 17-19) in which we are reminded of the trouble which Amalek caused our forefathers when they came out of Egypt. This special portion is called פָּרָשַׁת זָכוֹר (The Portion of Remembrance). It is because Haman was a descendant of the Amalekites that this portion is read on the Sabbath before פּוּרִים.

*13th:* תַּעֲנִית אֶסְתֵּר (Fast of Esther).

*14th:* פּוּרִים (Purim).

*15th:* שׁוּשַׁן פּוּרִים (Purim of Shushan).

On the Sabbath after פּוּרִים we read, in addition to the weekly portion of the Law, a special portion (Numbers, xix, 1-22), in which our forefathers were taught the great necessity of purifying themselves in readiness for the offering up of the Paschal lamb on the eve of Passover. Because this special portion deals with the Red Heifer, it is called פָּרָשַׁת פָּרָה (The Portion of the Red Heifer). It should remind us of the necessity of preparing ourselves for the Passover Festival.

On the last Sabbath of the month, or on the first day of the next month if it falls on a Sabbath, we read, in addition to the weekly portion of the Law, a special portion (Exodus, xii, 1-20), in which we are told that Nisan is to be the first month of the religious year, and are commanded concerning the Passover festival. This special portion is called פָּרָשַׁת הַחֹדֶשׁ (The Portion of the Month).

In a leap-year there is an extra month of Adar, which is called אֲדָר שֵׁנִי (Second Adar) The Fast of Esther, Purim, and the reading of the special portions, are then observed in the second Adar.

# PART II

## MORAL TEACHINGS OF THE RABBIS

## MORAL TEACHINGS OF THE RABBIS

THE Rabbis were occupied, during a period of almost a thousand years, in explaining the Laws of the Bible, many of which would otherwise have been far too difficult for us to thoroughly understand. We are not only indebted to them, however, for these explanations, but also for the great number of moral teachings which they have taught us, and which are made known to us in the form of sayings, or incidents, in their lives. These teachings have proved of very great value to me during the lessons in which I have endeavoured to instil in the minds of my pupils a love for, and a knowledge of, the various moral duties upon which such supreme importance is attached by our ancient faith. As they have been so well accepted by my pupils, and have borne such very good results, I am convinced that the inclusion of a selection of these sayings and incidents, all of which are to be found in either the Talmud or Midrash, will serve a most valuable moral purpose. Their teachings should be continually borne in mind and permitted to influence every thought and action.

### DUTY TOWARDS PARENTS

DAMAH, the son of Nethina, was a diamond merchant, and a very dutiful son. One of the precious stones which was attached to the priestly garments was once lost, and when the Priests were informed that Damah possessed a stone similar to the one which had been lost, they immediately went to him and offered a very large price for it. He consented to take the amount which they offered, and went into an adjoining room to bring the required stone. On entering the room, however, he found that his father was asleep with his foot resting on the chest which contained the stone; and so, without disturbing him, he returned to the Priests and explained that, for the moment, he was compelled to forgo the large profit which he could have earned, as otherwise he would have to disturb his father's rest. The matter being urgent, and as the Priests thought that he had invented an excuse in order to obtain a still larger price, he was offered a higher amount. 'No,' replied the dutiful son, 'I would not, even for the treasures of the world, disturb my father's rest.' When his father awoke, he brought them the stone, and was offered the amount which was mentioned on the second occasion, but he would not accept it. 'I will not exchange the satisfaction of having done my duty, for gold', he said. 'Give me the amount that you offered at first, and I will be satisfied.'

A child must love and honour his parents while they are living, and must love and respect them after they are dead; and as they loved and honoured God, so he must love and honour God, and thus make his parents live again in his own good deeds.

There are many ways in which honour is to be shown to parents. If they prefer a certain corner or have a certain chair upon which they sit, these are not to be used even when vacated by them. Thy must not be contradicted, and attention is to be shown them in every possible way

The honour and reverence due to parents are equal to the honour and reverence due to God; where the children honour their parents, there God dwells and there He is honoured.

## PRAYER

PRAYER is Israel's only weapon, a weapon inherited from our fathers, and a weapon tried in a thousand battles.

Prayer, without devotion, is like a body without life, and it is therefore better to pray a little with devotion, than very much without devotion.

The command to serve the Lord with all the heart has reference to prayer. Prayer is the service of the heart more than of the lips.

Prayer, as a means of intercession between God and ourselves, should only be resorted to after much preparation. Banish unworthy thoughts and material considerations from your mind before you commence to engage yourself in Prayer. Realise how small and feeble we are when compared with our Father in Heaven, and this will cause you to approach Him with feelings of humbleness and awe. Yet we should also feel a holy joy that He who is receiving our prayers is a Merciful and Almighty God, and we should feel confident of the fulfilment of such words as 'The Redeemer of Israel will fulfil the desire of them that fear Him. He will hear their cry and will save them. For the Lord will not forsake His people for His great name's sake.'

Our father Abraham said to the Most Holy, blessed be He: 'In the days when the Temple will no more exist and sacrifices will therefore be impossible, what shall serve as an atonement for the sins of my children (the people of the Jewish nation)?' 'They shall include in their daily prayers the portions of the Bible which deal with the laws of the sacrifices, and I will account it unto them as if they had performed the sacrifices themselves,' answered the Most Holy, blessed be He.

This should teach us the great necessity of devoting as much care and attention to the reciting of the Sacrificial Prayers as if we were performing the actual sacrifices themselves.

## REPENTANCE

Repent one day before thy death, and as thou knowest not which is the day, therefore repent each day lest thou wilt delay too long.

In three ways may we repent; by publicly confessing our sins, by heartfelt sorrow for sins which we have committed, and by good deeds, which act as sacrifices before our Heavenly Father.

Rabbi Meir had a very wicked neighbour, who caused him so much annoyance that the Rabbi one day prayed for his death. When his wife heard it, she reproved her husband with the words: 'Remember the teachings of your faith. Do not pray that the wicked should be destroyed, but rather that wickedness should be destroyed, and the wicked repent of their evil ways.'

Repentance will destroy an evil decree which is already signed and sealed.

The gates of prayer are sometimes open and sometimes closed, but the gates of repentance are always open.

The son of a king went away from home and turned to evil ways; so the king sent a messenger to him requesting him to return home. The son, however, replied that he was filled with too great a shame to return, and so the father again sent the messenger with the words: 'Should a son feel too much ashamed to return to his father?'

We should bear in mind that God is our Father, who is always ready to welcome us back when we have become estranged from Him because of our sinful actions. We should therefore return to Him in perfect repentance, and being assured that He is ready to accept that repentance.

## HILLEL AND SHAMMAI

Hillel, in addition to being a very learned Rabbi, possessed the virtues of humility and meekness in the highest degree; Shammai, though also a Rabbi of great learning, had a very hasty temper.

A heathen came to Shammai and said: ' I wish to become a convert to Judaism, but only on condition that thou wilt teach me the whole Law whilst I stand upon one leg.' The short-tempered Rabbi, offended at so unreasonable a request, drove the heathen away. He next went to Hillel and made the same request. Hillel answered him with the words: ' Remember, whatever thou dislikest thyself, do not unto thy neighbour. This is the essence of the Law, and everything else is but its explanation; now go and learn.' The heathen thanked him, and became a good and pious man.

Another heathen, passing a synagogue, heard the following words: ' And these are the garments which they shall make; a breast-plate, and an ephod, and a robe, and a broidered coat, a mitre and a girdle,' etc., etc. (Exodus, xxviii, 4). He immediately enquired for whom all these fine garments were intended? ' For the High Priest,' he was told. On hearing this, he went to Shammai, and said: ' Rabbi, I wish to become a convert to Judaism, but only on condition that I shall be made a High Priest.' Shammai again became offended at such an unreasonable request, and drove this heathen away also. He next went to Hillel and made the same request. This gentle Rabbi then replied to him: ' Hast thou ever known a king to be appointed without being first taught the rules of government? Whoever wishes to be High

Priest must first be taught the rules belonging to so dignified an office. Come then, and learn.' He then taught the heathen the eighteenth chapter of the fourth book of the Pentateuch, which is called Numbers. When they came to the words: 'And *the stranger* that cometh nigh shall be put to death' (verse 7), the heathen asked who was meant by *the stranger*? 'The name *stranger*', answered Hillel, 'applies to any person who is not a descendant of Aaron. Even David, the King of Israel, if he had dared to carry out this sacred duty, would have been punishable with death.' The heathen then thought to himself, 'If the greatest king of Israel was not thought worthy of filling this office, how should I, a poor miserable stranger, become worthy?' He therefore gave up the idea of becoming a High Priest, but continued to study, and afterwards became a member of that nation to whom God said: 'Ye shall be unto me a kingdom of priests' (Exodus, xix, 6). After some time Hillel, Shammai and the Jewish convert met together, and the grateful convert exclaimed: 'Shammai's harshness almost drove me from the world (meaning that if he had not become converted to Judaism his life would have been wasted); but Hillel's gentleness saved me. May all the blessings of God rest upon thy head, thou worthy teacher of Israel! for it is thou who hast brought me under the wings of the Divine presence.'

Hillel was never too proud to help, or speak, to the most ignorant and lowly of the common people in the streets, and he was, in this way, often able to do much good.

A man once had a wager with a friend that he could cause Hillel to become angry. He therefore came to Rabbi Hillel and called out: ‘ Where is Hillel? Where is Hillel? ’ purposely leaving out the title Rabbi. Hillel, who was preparing for his bath, covered himself with a cloak, and with his usual good patience, asked the man what he wanted. ‘ I want to know ’, answered the man, ‘ why the Babylonians have round heads? ’ Hillel was himself a Babylonian, and the question was therefore a direct insult to him, but although he had been called from his bath to answer such a very foolish question, and had then been insulted, he answered: ‘ An important question indeed; the reason is because they have no experienced nurses.’ The man went away, but soon returned and again called out: ‘ Where is Hillel? Where is Hillel? ’ The Rabbi answered: ‘ What dost thou want, my son? ’ ‘ I want to know ’, said the man, ‘ why the Tamorians have weak eyes? ’ ‘ Because they live in a sandy country; the sand flying in their eyes causes soreness ’, answered Hillel. The man went away disappointed, but decided to have yet a third attempt, and so he again returned and called: ‘ Where is Hillel? I want Hillel! ’ ‘ What is thy pleasure now? ’ asked Hillel mildly. ‘ I want to know ’ answered the man, ‘ why the Africans have broad feet? ’ ‘ Because ’, said Hillel, ‘ they live in a marshy land.’ ‘ I would desire to ask thee many more questions', said the man, 'but I fear thou wilt be angry.' 'Fear nothing,' said the meek and patient Rabbi, 'ask as many questions as it pleases thee; and if I am able I will answer them.' The man was astonished at Hillel's patience, and fearing to lose his money, he decided that the only chance which now remained to him was to insult Hillel to his face, and he therefore asked: 'Art thou the Hillel who is styled the Prince of the Israelites?' Hillel replied that he was so called (as he was the most honoured and exalted of the Israelites in his generation). 'Well, then,' said the man, 'if so, may Israel not produce many persons like thee.' 'And why not?' asked Hillel, very much surprised. 'Because', said the man, 'through thy patience I have lost four hundred Zuzim.' 'Thy money is not entirely lost', said the Rabbi with a smile, 'because it will teach thee to be more careful in the future, and not to make such foolish wagers. Besides, it is far better that thou shouldst lose thy money, than that Hillel should lose his patience.'

## HEAVENLY JUDGMENT

CONSIDER three things and thou wilt never fall into sin; remember that there is above thee an All-seeing Eye, an All-hearing Ear, and a record of all thy actions.

When Rabbi Jochanan, the son of Zaccai, who was a man of great learning and piety, was taken ill, his pupils visited him. They found their teacher dying, and were greatly surprised to observe his eyes filled with tears, as he had continually lectured to them about the vanity of this world, the immortality of the soul, and the great rewards which the souls of the righteous will enjoy after they have passed from this earthly life. They therefore asked Rabbi Jochanan to explain to them why he was now filled with such feelings of sadness. Their pious teacher answered them: 'Suppose I were to be brought before the court of justice of some great King, who after all is but flesh and blood, here to-day, to-morrow in the grave; whose anger, however fearful, cannot last for ever; who might indeed kill me but could not rob me of a future life; nay, whom perhaps I might win over with words, or bribe with money or valuables; nevertheless, I should tremble, be afraid, and weep. But now I am about to be brought before the fearful presence and majesty of the King of Kings; before Him who lives and will live for ever. His just anger may be eternal; He may doom me to everlasting punishment; and should He condemn me to death, it is a death without further hope. Nor can I calm Him with words, nor bribe Him with money. Have I not cause to weep?' The disciples, knowing the piety of their dying teacher, pleaded with him to grant a last blessing upon them. 'May you fear God', said the Rabbi, 'as much as one fears an earthly king, who is after all made of flesh and blood.' 'Rabbi,' said his disciples, 'is this all, and no more?' 'O!' replied the dying Rabbi, 'may it be even so! Think, my children, how intensely anxious a person is to hide his faults from his fellow man? Would any person be guilty of a crime if he was certain it would be known? Remember, therefore, that nothing can be hidden from the All-seeing Eye of God, and lead a faultless life.'

An exceedingly learned Rabbi, called Rabbeinu Hakadosh, was once asked: 'When a man dies and the body decays, how is it possible for God to judge the man?' He replied by relating the following story: 'A king once appointed two men to look after his orchard. One was blind and the other was lame, but as they were only required to keep robbers away, they were good enough. One day the lame man noticed a bunch of sweet, delicious grapes, and so he arranged with the blind man that he should carry him to the place where the grapes were hanging, and they would share them. The next day the king, who had noticed the grapes, entered the orchard to obtain them, but he found that they had vanished. He therefore accused the men of the theft, but the lame man pleaded, "How can my Lord accuse me when I am lame and cannot move from this spot?" The blind man pleaded, "How can you accuse me when I am blind and therefore did not even know of the grapes?" The king then ordered the lame man to be placed on the back of the blind man and he punished them together, as if they were both of one body. The soul and the body are both necessary to work together before a sin is committed, and so the Most Holy, blessed be He, will judge them together.'

There was a king who invited all his servants to a party but did not say at what hour it would begin. Some of the servants went home and put on their nicest clothes and awaited the time when the king would call them; the others waited until the king would announce the hour. But the servants were unexpectedly called, and those that were ready were welcomed to the party, whilst those who had waited until it proved too late were turned away in disgrace.

We will all be called before God, at some time or other, and will have to give an account for all our actions. We should therefore prepare ourselves while there is yet time by obeying the will of God, and sincerely repenting anything which we have done or said which we know is displeasing before Him.

## HOSPITALITY

LET thy house be wide open to everyone, and let the poor be cheerfully received within thy walls.

When the son of Rabbi Gameliel was married he invited three Rabbis, named Eliezer, Joshuah and Zadig, to the marriage-feast. Gameliel, although one of the most honoured men amongst the Israelites, himself waited on his guests, and pouring out a cup of wine, handed it to Eliezer, who politely refused it. Gameliel then handed it to Joshuah, who accepted it. Eliezer then said to Joshuah: 'Shall we indeed sit and allow so highly honoured and great a man to wait upon us?' 'Why not?' replied Joshuah. 'Did not a man who was even greater than Gameliel do so long before him? Was not our father Abraham a very great man? Yet even he waited upon his guests, as it is written: "And he (Abraham) stood by them (the guests) whilst they were eating." Perhaps you may think that he did so only because he knew them to be angels; it is not so; he must have supposed them to be travellers, as otherwise he would not have offered them either water to wash their feet or food to satisfy their hunger. Why then shall we prevent our kind host from imitating so excellent an example?' 'I can tell you of one who is still very much greater than Abraham, who doeth the same,' exclaimed Rabbi Zadig. 'How long shall we spend in being engaged in declaring the praises of created beings, and meanwhile neglect the glory of our Heavenly Father, the Creator of all? Even the Most Holy, blessed be He, is continually acting as our host by causing the winds to blow, the clouds to gather, and the rain to fall. He causes the earth to become fruitful, and provides us each day with food and other necessities. Why then shall we hinder our kind host, Gameliel, from following so glorious an example?'

He who does an act of kindness to those who are really in need will have a greater reward than that which was granted to Abraham, who showed hospitality to angels. He stood under a tree and waited on the three strangers whilst they ate and drank, and God rewarded his children, while they were in the desert, with manna and quails for food, and caused water to spring forth from a rock to satisfy their thirst; while the cloud of Divine Glory watched over them. The angels needed nothing, and yet the Israelites were granted such a great reward in return for the hospitality which was shown towards them; how much greater will be the reward granted in return for the hospitality which we show towards the poor and needy, who are in such great need.

## CLEANLINESS

### A Holy Duty

Hillel was one day accompanied home, after ending his lecture at the College, by some of his pupils. They asked him what he now intended doing, and he replied: ‘ I am now about to perform a holy duty.’ The pupils then enquired what duty he intended to perform, and were told that he was about to bathe himself. ‘ Is that a holy duty ? ’ they enquired. ‘ Most certainly,’ he replied. ‘ If the statues of the kings which stand on view must be kept clean and washed very often, how much more should I, who have been created in the image of God, keep my body clean ? ’

## VAIN DESIRES

‘ You teach ’, said the Emperor Trajan to Rabbi Joshua, ‘ that your god is everywhere, and boast that He dwells amongst your nation. I should like to see Him.’ ‘ God’s presence is most certainly everywhere,’ replied the Rabbi, ‘ but He cannot be seen; as the eye of a living person cannot behold His glory.' The Emperor, however, insisted in his desire. 'Very well,' said the Rabbi, 'let us first try to look at one of his creations.' He then took the Emperor into the open air at noon time, when the sun was shining at its brightest, and asked him to look at the sun. 'I cannot,' answered the Emperor, 'its light and brightness dazzles me.' 'You are unable,' said the Rabbi, 'to look at the light even of one of God's creations; how then can you expect to be capable of looking at the Majestic light of the glory of its Creator? Would not such a sight utterly destroy you?'

The Emperor Hadrian one day told Rabbi Joshua that he intended giving a banquet to God. The Rabbi answered him: 'But your Majesty, the number of God's Court is so very great that with all your riches you will be unable to carry out your desire.' The Emperor persisted in his intention, and the Rabbi then told him that it would be but right that he should prepare his banquet on the sea-shore, as the sea, which is one of God's mightiest servants, would then be able to partake of it. Hadrian therefore prepared a banquet and invited thousands of people, and the tables were filled with the most costly dishes. But, as the Rabbi knew would happen, the sea swept the whole banquet away, and it was only then that Hadrian realised how foolish and impossible was his desire, as the sea, which was only one of God's servants, had sent forth a few waves which had been enough to destroy the whole feast.

Jealousy and conceit are vices which are the cause of much trouble and suffering; and foolish demands should never gain our consent or agreement. This is explained in the following tale:

The serpent's tail had, for a very long time, followed in the way which the head had gone, and all went on well. One day the tail began to be dissatisfied with following the head, and therefore said: 'I have long, with great dissatisfaction, noticed thy unjust proceedings. In all our journey it was thou that leadest, whilst I, like a mean servant, was obliged to follow behind. Thou didst appear everywhere first, whilst I was compelled to remain behind. Was this just? Was it fair? Am I not a member of the same body? Why should not I have its management as well as thou?' 'Thou!' exclaimed the head, 'thou silly tail, desirest thou to manage the body? Thou hast neither eyes to see dangers, nor ears to be warned, nor brains to prevent danger; dost thou not understand that it is even for thy own advantage that I should lead?' 'For my advantage, indeed!' exclaimed the tail. 'This is the language of everyone who wishes to wield power. They all pretend to rule for the benefit of their slaves; but I will no longer allow such a state of affairs. I insist upon taking the lead.' 'Very well,' replied the head, 'be it so. Lead on.' The tail proudly took the lead, and its first action was to drag the body into a filthy ditch. It struggled hard, crawled along, and with great effort got out again; but the body was thickly covered with dirt and filth. Its next action was to get entangled amongst thorns. The pain was great, the whole body ached, and the more it struggled the deeper became the wounds. Now it would have ended its career had not the head come to its assistance; but the tail still persisted in leading. It marched on, and most unfortunately crept into a fiery furnace. Very soon it began to feel the terrific heat, and the whole body was terribly tortured with pain. The head again hastened to the help of the tail, but it was too late ; the tail was already burnt, and the fire, reaching the vital organs of the body, caused the ruin of the head as well.

If the tail had not been jealous and conceited, and if the head had not given way to the foolish demands of the tail, all would have continued to be well. This tale should teach us the dangers of these vices, and should impress upon us how firm we must be not to allow ourselves to be swept from the right course by the force of public opinion.

## UGLINESS

### Not a Crime

Rabbi Joshua, the son of Chananyah, was a very clever man, and was greatly loved by all people; but he was very ugly. He was very often present in the king's court, and a princess once asked him: 'How comes it that such glorious wisdom is enclosed in so mean a vessel ? ' The Rabbi, quite unperturbed, asked her to tell him in what sort of vessels her father kept his wine. 'Why, in earthen vessels, to be sure,' she replied. 'O!' exclaimed the Rabbi, 'but that is the way that ordinary people do; a king's wine should be kept in more precious vessels.' The princess, thinking him to be in earnest, ordered that a quantity of wine should be emptied out of the earthen vessels into gold and silver vessels; but, to her great surprise, she found that the wine had, in a very short time, become sour and unfit to drink. 'Very good advice, indeed, Rabbi Joshua, hast thou given me!' said the princess the next time she saw the Rabbi. 'Do you know that the wine became sour and spoilt?' 'Thou art then convinced', said the Rabbi, 'that wine keeps best in plain or mean vessels. It is even so with wisdom.' 'But', continued the princess, 'I know many people who are both wise and handsome.' 'True,' replied the Rabbi, 'but they would, most probably, be still wiser were they less beautiful, as beauty is most often accompanied by vanity.'

Despise not the deformed, as their defects are not of their own seeking, and why shouldst thou add insult to misfortune?

Despise not any creature; the most insignificant is the work of the Most Holy, blessed be He.

Rabbi Eliezer, returning from his teacher's place of study to his native town, was overjoyed with the great amount of knowledge he had gained. On his way he met a very ugly man, who was also travelling to the same town. The man greeted the Rabbi with the words: ' Peace be upon thee, Rabbi.' Eliezer, instead of returning the greeting, said: ' Are the people of your town all as ugly as you are ? ' The man, angered at the insult, replied: ' I do not know; but you had better make enquiries of the great Artist that made me.' The Rabbi, ashamed of his error, pleaded with the man to forgive the insult, but he answered: ' No ! Go first to the Artist that made me, and tell him, Great Artist, O ! what an ugly vessel hast thou made ! ' Eliezer continued to plead for pardon, but it was in vain. Meanwhile, they arrived at the town, and the Rabbi was met by a large crowd of people, who welcomed him with the words: ' Peace be upon thee, Rabbi ! Welcome our Instructor ! ' ' Whom do you call Rabbi ? ' asked the man. The people pointed to Eliezer. ' And him you honour with the name of Rabbi ? ' continued the man. ' O! May Israel not produce many like him ! ' He then told the people what had happened on the way, and they answered him : ' He has done wrong, and realises it, therefore forgive him; for he is a great man, very well versed in the Law.' The man then forgave him, and explained that his long refusal had only been meant to impress the error on the Rabbi's mind. The learned Eliezer thanked him; and whilst he held out his own conduct as a warning to the people, he justified the man's action by saying that although a person should always be ready to offer pardon, yet to insult poverty or natural defects is a very serious sin, and one that we cannot expect to be readily pardoned.

## MERCY

We best honour God when we try to imitate Him; as He is filled with tender mercy and gracious love, so should we be filled with these divine feelings.

Whosoever showeth mercy to mankind will himself be shown mercy from God; but whosoever lacketh mercy for mankind will himself lack mercy from God.

By three signs can we recognise the members of the Jewish race: a tender heart, self-respect, and practical benevolence.

Underneath the wings of the Seraphim are stretched the arms of divine mercy, ever ready to receive sinners.

Our mercy should also be extended to those of our enemies who are in trouble, and we should not rejoice at their distress. We are told that at the time when the Egyptians were drowning in the Red Sea the angels in heaven were about to sing songs of rejoicing before God. The Most Holy, blessed be He, stopped them, and said: 'Behold, my creatures are perishing in the sea, yet you wish to sing songs of delight.' If the Most Holy, blessed be He, felt mercy towards the wicked Egyptians, consider how readily we should feel mercy towards our enemies who are most certainly not as wicked as they were.

## ISRAEL

EVERY nation has its special guardians, but Israel is guarded by God Himself. No one is needed to act as peacemaker between Israel, who are God's chosen people, and the Almighty God.

When the Israelites were first driven into exile, oaths were administered by Heaven to both the Israelites and the Gentiles. The Israelites swore before God that they would never unite into one band to recover by force their freedom and their land; but that they would prove loyal to the countries where they would chance to dwell, and that they would never rebel against them. The Gentile nations swore before God that they would never subject the Israelites to such oppression as would prove too great for them to bear.

Some people were travelling in a boat and one of them commenced to bore a hole in the bottom of it. The other people strongly protested against his action, but he replied that he was only boring a hole under his own seat, and it was therefore no concern of theirs. But the people explained to him that it was not only his concern, as when the sea would rush into the boat through the hole under his seat, they would all be drowned.

This story can impress upon us that every Israelite is responsible for the honour of his nation; as if one Israelite commits an offence, the blame is not only suffered by that Israelite, but his nation is also blamed. One Israelite is therefore responsible for the other.

The punishments that come upon Israel are greater than those that come on the other peoples of the world, because those that are nearest to God are bound to be more holy than those that are far off. To them were given more laws, and from them more is expected. 'In those that are near Me I will be sanctified.'

Israel has been compared to the sand of the seashore. Men take of the sand and cast it into a fiery furnace, and it comes out clear and bright, and they make glass vessels of it through which the light shines. So Israel is cast into the fiery furnace of trouble and persecution, and not only are they saved to come out alive, but they are purified and are joined closer together, and help mankind to see the light of Heaven.

Just as the palm tree will produce fine dates along with some that are bad, and therefore not fit to be gathered, so among the people of Israel some are pious and learned in the Law of God, while others are wicked, stupid, and ignorant.

In another way Israel may be likened to a palm tree. Nothing that grows on the palm tree is useless. It bears dates for food; the branches serve for shade, and are used for Lulavim (the palm branches which are used during the Feast of Tabernacles); the fibres are made into ropes; while the wood is used for the beams of houses. Thus, in Israel, no one is without his aim in life, and his proper work or duty. Some are very learned in Scripture, others in the Mishna, Talmud, or Midrash. The aims of others are good works and charity; while others have lower, but not less useful, work in the world. But as the central stem, the heart of the palm tree, always grows up straight towards Heaven, so the heart of all people, and every separate person, should be constantly turned towards their Father who is in Heaven.

If all nations, as King David said, praise the Lord, how much more is it incumbent upon the Israelite to praise the Lord, for the wonderful help which He has granted to the Jewish nation.

Can it be in any way doubted that an Israelite is forbidden to practise all falseness, lying or dishonest dealing of any kind, if we bear in mind the words of the prophet: 'The remnant of Israel shall not do iniquity nor speak lies; neither shall a deceitful tongue be found in their mouth; for they shall feed and lie down and none shall make them afraid' (Zephaniah, iii, 13).

## HUMILITY

From the Almighty God Himself we learn humility. He did not choose the highest mountain upon which to give His commandments. He called to Moses from a lowly bush, and not from a lofty tree. When He spoke to Elijah He allowed the wind to roar, the earth to tremble, and the fire to flash forth ; but for His medium He chose ' a still small voice '.

The prayers of a proud hard-hearted man are never heard.

If you know one who is in the habit of greeting you, practice humility by trying to greet him first.

It is much better to be humble by nature than to be forced to become humble because of shame or punishment.

For three years there had been dispute between the schools of Shamai and Hillel, regarding whose decision should be final. Then a heavenly voice was heard proclaiming: ' The pupils of both these schools are occupied with the words of the Living God; yet the decision of the pupils of Hillel's school regarding religious laws is to be final.' The reason given for the preference of Hillel's school over the school of Shamai was that they were modest and humble. They always considered well the decisions of the school of Shamai side by side with their own views, and were not too proud to give way to the opposed views if they were well grounded. Thus we have the lesson of humility put before us. He whose ambition in life is to be popular among men must possess the qualities of meekness and humbleness. Such people are exalted and beloved by everyone.

That humility is a divine quality is taught us when we observe that whenever the greatness of God is spoken of in the Bible, there you will also find His humility and meekness. Thus you will find it written, 'God is the God of gods and the Lord of lords' (Deuteronomy, x, 17), and this is immediately followed by the words: 'He loveth the stranger, giving him food and garments' (Deuteronomy, x, 18). It is also written that He is 'The high and lofty One that inhabits eternity' (Isaiah, lvii, 15), and this is continued with the words: 'He also dwelleth with him that is of a penitent and humble spirit.' The Psalmist who proclaims 'Extol Him who rideth upon the Heavens' (Psalm lxviii, 5), accompanies these words with the expression: 'A father of the fatherless and a judge of the widows is God in His holy dwelling.' Happy is the man who, striving to follow God, becomes possessed of such a quality.

Whosoever runs after greatness, greatness runs away from him; but he who runs from greatness, greatness will follow him.

What a crown of glory man can make for himself if he possesses meekness, humility and a kindly nature.

## MAN

God gave man his spirit in a state of perfect purity, and it is man's duty to restore it, when called upon to do so, in the condition in which he received it.

A good man is guided by his better qualities which check any passing thought of evil, but a wicked man stifles his passing thoughts of any good deed and gives full sway to his evil inclinations.

The man who lives in a large town and keeps away from its baseness and sinfulness, the poor man who finds something valuable and restores it to its owner, and the rich man who gives charity in secret, these are possessed of praiseworthy characters.

Man should rather turn a carcass in the open street, than turn from his given word. He should be ready to skin a carcass, if need be, in order to earn his bread, and not despise such work because he regards it as beneath his dignity, his education or his high birth. There can be no shame in earning an honest wage, whatever the work may be.

There are certain men who richly deserve to be despised: a poor man who is haughty, a rich man who performs a mean act in order to gain some money, and an old man whose mind, manners or morals are corrupted.

A man may feel some deep misgiving once or twice in committing a sin; but let him persist in that sin, and he will become accustomed to look upon it as of little consequence; later he will look upon it as no sin at all.

Whether a man be strong or weak, rich or poor, wise or foolish, depends mostly on circumstances that surround him from the time of his birth; but whether a man be good or bad, righteous or wicked, depends on his own free will.

## THE TONGUE

RABBI GAMELIEL ordered his servant to bring something good from the market, and so he brought a tongue. At another time he told him to bring back something which was not necessarily good, and he again brought a tongue. 'Why did you bring a tongue on both occasions?' asked the Rabbi. 'Because', answered the servant, 'it is the cause of both good and evil. If it is used for a good purpose there is nothing better, but if it is used for an evil purpose there is nothing worse.'

Four kinds of persons shall not enter Paradise: the scoffer, the liar, the hypocrite, and the slanderer.

The penalty which a liar has to pay is that he is not believed even when he is speaking the truth.

'What care', said Rabbi Zimra, 'has not the All-Wise Creator bestowed on the chief organ of speech? All the other chief members of the human body are protected, and are placed either upright or bending. The tongue, however, is placed internally and in a lying position, in order that it might remain quiet and steady. Still more, in order that it might be kept within its natural bounds, He has surrounded it with two walls; one of ivory (the teeth), and the other of softer substance (the lips). Further, to lessen its great eagerness to move, he has surrounded it with an ever-flowing stream (the salivary glands). Yet, notwithstanding all this Divine care, what mischief does it not do? How many burning tortures does it not raise? and what destructions does it not cause?

A Persian King was once ordered by his physicians to drink the milk of a lioness, and one of his servants offered to obtain the required milk. After many dangerous experiences the servant succeeded in obtaining the milk, and commenced to journey homewards. While on his journey, he fell into a deep sleep, during which the different organs of his body began to quarrel with one another regarding which of them had most helped to bring his quest to a successful result. The feet claimed that without doubt they alone had brought about the success, as without them the servant could not have set out on his mission. The hands would not allow the credit to the feet, but claimed that without the help that they had given it would have been impossible to obtain the required milk. The eyes claimed that without them neither the feet nor the hands would have served any purpose; whilst the heart claimed the credit because it had induced the servant to undertake the mission. Lastly, the tongue put in its claim by asking: 'What would all your actions amount to without me?' 'You!' scornfully replied the other organs, and merely laughed at the very idea of the tongue claiming any credit in the matter. The tongue became angry at their scorn and laughter, and said: 'Very well, you shall find out my powers, but it will be to your sorrow.' When the servant arrived at the king's court and presented the milk, he said: 'I have brought your Majesty the dog's milk.' The King became very angry and ordered the servant to be put to death. All the organs of the body now trembled, but the tongue only laughed and said: 'Did I not tell you that my power was far greater than your united powers? Are you now ready to agree to my great power? I will save you from the immediate danger which threatens.' The servant now requested to be again brought before the King, and he then pleaded for his life, but the King replied: 'You have yourself stated it to be dog's milk.' The servant then replied: 'I confess that I have made a most unfortunate mistake, as although you will find, by testing, that the milk is truly from a lioness, yet unfortunately, in my great haste to present it to you, I accidentally spoke the wrong name.'

The King now ordered the milk to be tested, and upon finding it to be the milk of a lioness, he freed the servant and rewarded him. Then the organs of the body agreed that life and death are in the power of the tongue. You must remember, at all times, the great power of the tongue, both for good and evil, and therefore put your whole heart into the words which you say in your prayers, three times daily: 'O my God! guard my tongue from evil and my lips from speaking deceitfully.'

The serpent was once asked: ‘What profit hast thou in robbing other people of their lives? The lion kills and eats; the wolf strangles and devours; other savage beasts destroy to satisfy their ravenous appetite. But thou alone strikest the innocent victim, and spittest thy deadly venom without any other satisfaction, except the fiendish pleasure of destroying!’ ‘And why do you ask me?’ replied the serpent. ‘Rather ask the slanderer. What pleasure has he in scattering his poisonous words and mortally wounding those who have never injured him? Besides, I kill only those that are near to me; but he destroys and injures at a distance. He scatters his vile slander here, and it often inflicts deadly wounds at a distant place.’

Slanderous words are always dangerous. Once spoken, they can never be recalled, as such words are quickly passed on from one person to another; they are the cause of great suffering and anxiety, although the slanderer may not have intended them to be so.

## THE AGED PLANTER

A Rabbi was passing through a field when he saw a very old man planting an oak tree. He said to him: ‘Why are you planting that oak tree. Surely you do not expect to live long enough to see it grow up?’ ‘Ah,’ replied the man, ‘if my forefathers had not planted trees we should not now enjoy their shade or their fruit. What my fathers did for me, that will I do for the future generations.’

We should not only strive to do such things as will

benefit ourselves, but we must also be ready to perform such things as will be of benefit to other people.

The Emperor Hadrian once noticed an old man digging a large trench in order to plant some fig trees. 'If you had spent your younger years to more useful purpose, then you would not have needed to work so hard now when you are old,' said the Emperor to the old man. 'I have indeed spent my younger years to very good purpose, but I will certainly not allow that to cause me to neglect my later years,' answered the old man. 'How old are you, good man?' asked the Emperor. 'A hundred years,' was the reply. 'What!' exclaimed the Emperor. 'You claim to be a hundred years old, and yet you are planting trees. Can you then hope ever to enjoy the fruits of your labour?' 'Great King,' answered the old man, 'yes, I most certainly do hope; if God will permit, then I may even eat of the fruit of these very trees; if not, then my children will have the pleasure of eating from them. Have not my forefathers planted trees for me, and shall I not do the same for my children?' The Emperor was pleased with the honest old man's reply, and so he said: 'Well, old man, if ever you live to see the fruits of these trees, let me know it. Remember to do as I have said, my good old man,' and the Emperor then left him. The old man did live long enough to see the fruits of his labour. The trees flourished and bore excellent fruit. As soon as they were sufficiently ripe, he gathered the most choice figs, put them into a basket, and marched off towards the house of the Emperor. Hadrian happened to look out of one of the windows of the palace; seeing a man bent with age, and with a basket on his shoulders, standing near the gate, he ordered him to be led before his presence. 'What is thy pleasure, old man?' demanded the Emperor. 'May it please your majesty', answered the old man 'to remember once seeing a very old man planting some trees, when you desired him, if ever he should gather the fruit, to let you know. I am that old man, and this is the fruit of those very trees which you saw me planting. May it please you graciously to accept them, as a humble tribute of gratitude for the interest which your majesty has taken in me.' The Emperor, pleased to see such an instance of extreme old age accompanied by the full use of the powers of body and mind, desired the old man to be seated, and ordering the basket to be emptied of the fruit and to be filled with gold, gave it to him as a present. Some of the Emperor's ministers, who were amazed at what had taken place, exclaimed: 'Is it possible that our great Emperor should show so much honour to a miserable Jew!' (Hadrian dealt most cruelly with the Jews, as he desired utterly to destroy them.) 'Why should I not honour him whom God has honoured?' replied the Emperor. 'Look at his age, and imitate his example.' He then dismissed the old man, who went home highly pleased and delighted.

## MERITED PUNISHMENTS

When the old man (about whom you have read in the last tale) came home and showed the present of gold which he had received from the Emperor, the people were all astonished. Amongst the people whom curiosity had brought to his house, there was a very jealous woman, who, seeing so much treasure obtained for a basket of figs, imagined that the Emperor must be very fond of that fruit. She therefore ran home as quickly as possible, and, after heaping reproaches on her husband for wasting valuable time by delaying, asked him: 'Have you not heard that the Emperor is very fond of figs? Go! Do not delay any longer. Take some to him, and he will also present you with gold, as he did our neighbour.' The foolish husband took a large sack filled with figs on his shoulder, and after much trouble and feeling very tired, he at last arrived at the gates of the palace, and demanded to be admitted to the Emperor. Being asked what he wanted, he answered that, as he was given to understand that the Emperor was very fond of figs, he had brought a whole sackfull, for which he expected a great reward. The officer on duty reported the man's words to the Emperor, who could not help smiling at the folly and impertinence of the man. 'Very well,' he replied to the officer, 'the fool shall have his reward. Let him remain where he is, and let every person who enters the gate take one of the figs and throw it at his face, till they are all gone; then let him depart.' The order was faithfully fulfilled. The foolish man, abused, pelted, and mocked, instead of wishing for gold, wished only to see the bottom of his sack. After long and patient waiting, and not before he was in great pain, was his wish fulfilled. The sack became empty, and the poor man was permitted to leave the gates of the palace, and make his way home, feeling very sorrowful and disheartened. His wife had been spending the time, until his return, by forming plans how best to enjoy the expected treasure; she had decided how many gowns, cloaks and hats she would purchase, and felt great inward joy when she saw in her mind's eye how well she would look when she would wear them. The poor man at last arrived home, and although she immediately noticed that his sack was empty, she imagined that his pockets at least were full. Without giving him a chance to take his breath, or giving him the usual greeting, she hastily asked him to tell her exactly what good luck he had enjoyed. 'Have patience, you foolish woman,' replied the enraged man, 'have patience, and I will tell you. I have had both great and good luck. My great luck was that I took to the Emperor figs and not peaches, otherwise I should not have lived to return but should have been stoned to death; and my good luck was that the figs were ripe, otherwise I would have left my brains behind me.'

Rabbi Huna dealt in wine, of which he kept a large store. He had the misfortune to have four hundred barrels of his wine spoiled and unfit for sale. Rabbi

Jehudah and some of the wise men went to offer him their consolation. After expressing their sorrow at his heavy loss, they begged him to examine and review his general conduct. 'My friends,' said Rabbi Huna, who was really a most pious man, 'do you then suspect me of having committed a sin deserving of so severe a punishment?' 'And do you then imagine that the Divine Judge punisheth without a correct cause?' answered the wise men. 'Well, then,' said Rabbi Huna, 'if you know anything wrong of me, you had better tell me.' His learned friends then told him that they had been informed that he neglected to give his gardeners the branches of the vines which were due to them. 'It is quite true,' answered Rabbi Huna, 'but what crime is there in that? Know ye not that they generally take much more than is due to them?' 'True,' said the wise men; 'but do you forget what the proverb says, that he who steals from the dishonest, shares their plunder?' By these words they meant that we must act honestly, even towards those who injure us. Rabbi Huna, although rich, powerful, and learned was not ashamed to acknowledge his fault. He corrected his past mistakes, and thanked the wise men for the moral lesson which they had taught him.

Rabbi Joshua happened once to lodge at the house of a widow. She prepared something for his dinner, and, being hungry, he ate it all (instead of leaving some for the servants, as was the custom at that time). The next day he did the same. The third day the widow, wishing to make him realise his mistakes of the previous two days, so over-seasoned the food which she had prepared for him that it proved impossible to be eaten, and so he made a meal of bread. ‘Why do you not eat of what has been prepared for you?’ asked the widow. ‘Because I am not hungry,’ he answered, as he did not wish to vex the widow by telling her that the meal was not eatable. ‘If you are not hungry, why do you eat bread? Do people eat bread by way of desert?’ she asked with a meaning smile. ‘But’, she continued, ‘I can perhaps guess the reason. You are leaving this food for the poor servants whom you forgot yesterday and the day before. Is it not so, Rabbi?’ Rabbi Joshua then understood that the food had been over-seasoned in order that he should be taught a lesson, and readily, most humbly, acknowledged his fault.

## HONESTY

Rabbi Simon once bought a camel from a non-Jew, and while removing the saddle he discovered a band of diamonds hidden under it. His disciples, not knowing that he had already noticed it, exclaimed: ‘Rabbi! Rabbi! The blessing of God maketh rich!’ meaning that the gift of diamonds was an act of God. ‘Take them back to the man from whom I purchased the animal,’ said the virtuous Rabbi. ‘He sold me a camel, not precious stones.’ The diamonds were accordingly returned, to the no small surprise of the owner, but the Rabbi preserved the much more valuable jewels of Honesty and Uprightness.

The most worthy crown is a good reputation.

Your neighbour's goods should be regarded by you as precious to him as your goods are to you.

Rabbi Safra had a jewel for which he desired ten pieces of gold. Several dealers saw the jewel and offered five pieces of gold. The Rabbi would not sell it at their price, and so they departed. On second thoughts, however, he decided to accept the price offered by the dealers. The next day, just as he was in the midst of his prayers, the dealers unexpectedly returned, and said: ' Sir, we have come to you again to do business after all. Do you now wish to sell the jewel for the price we offered you yesterday? ' But the Rabbi did not reply (as it would not be right for a person to divert his mind from the worship and service of God in order to converse with another person). ' Well, well; be not angered; we will add another two pieces,' said the dealers, thinking that the Rabbi remained silent because he was angry with them, and as he still remained silent, they continued: ' Then be it as you said, and we will give you the ten pieces as you asked yesterday.' By this time the Rabbi had ended his prayer, and said: ' Sirs, I was at prayers and my mind was so engrossed in what I was saying that I did not hear what you were saying to me. But if you have come for the jewel, then I have decided upon selling it at the price you offered me yesterday.' The dealers paid the five pieces of gold and received the jewel.

He who reaps a benefit from a thief, by helping him to reap the profit of the theft by buying from him what he steals, is himself thoroughly dishonest, and the more guilty of the two. This is explained in the Midrash as follows: A very wise prince once made a law that the receiver of stolen property should be hanged, and the thief go free. This caused great surprise to many people, but others understood the meaning and reason of the law. The prince, anxious to teach the people the wisdom of his command, ordered all his subjects to meet him on a large field, which he had prepared for the occasion by having a number of holes pierced in the ground. The people gathered together, as they had been ordered, and pieces of meat were strewn all over the ground, and a few weasels were let loose. In a short time the weasels seized the meat and disappeared down the holes. On the following day the people were again ordered to gather on the field, which was again strewn with meat, but every hole had this time been stopped up. The weasels were again let loose, and immediately seized the meat and looked for some hole where they could run, but finding that there were no holes in which they could eat the meat, they dropped it. 'Do you now understand', said the prince to the people, 'why I made such a law? Theft can only continue when the thief has a place where he can take his stolen goods and sell them, or exchange them for something he needs. If the thief did not have such a place, it would prove useless for him to steal, and the receiver is therefore worse than the thief.'

## SIN AND SLANDER

He who performs sins in secret, thinking that there is no one who is aware of it, is guilty of the sin of banishing the presence of God, as he does not believe that God is present everywhere, and knows everything which we do or even think.

He who is a sinner, and causes others to sin, for such a person there is no hope of repentance, as it will be denied to him.

The man who says: ' I will sin, and will later repent of the sin,' will never repent.

There are sins which few men escape; slander of some sort; if he has prayed with devotion, he considers that he is entitled to be rewarded for it and puts in a sort of claim on God; and thoughts of an impure nature.

To slander is to murder, as the slanderer sheds the blood of him whom he slanders.

While slander is strictly forbidden there may arise cases where exposure is a necessity. The unveiling of a bad man's character, even though much must be said against him, cannot in any way be called slander. Such a person is a hypocrite; one who is a worker of iniquity in private, and poses as a good and righteous man in public. The unmasking of such a man is a praiseworthy act.

The way of the slanderer is to begin with faint praise of his victim, knowing that his hurtful and damaging words will then have a much better chance of being listened to.

Consider how harmful is the sin of slander. The spies chiefly slandered the cities, or in other words only bricks and mortar, yet they were punished so severely; how much greater, therefore, will be the punishment meted out to the slanderer who speaks words of slander against his fellow man ?

A slanderer injures three persons: himself (as he reaps a sin), him that receives the slander (as he reaps a sin for listening to slander), and the person who is slandered.

## CHARACTER

THERE are three crowns: that of the Law, the priesthood, and royalty; but the crown of a good name is higher than all of them.

Three names are given to a person: one by his parents, another by the world, and the third by his works; which of these three names is the best ? King Solomon gives us the answer when he says: ‘ A good name is better than the sweetest oil.’

As a tree is known by its fruit, so is a man known by his deeds.

The righteous man is a pillar upon which all the world rests.

## FEAR OF GOD

God has no greater treasure than the fear of Him. He bestows this on no one; it is therefore free to all and every person can possess it.

He who possesses knowledge of the words of God, but not of the fear of Him, is like a man who makes a door for a house without possessing the house to fix the door into.

The fear of God should ever be a man's first care.

Rabbi Eleazer said: ' He who is guided by righteousness and justice in all his doings may justly claim to have copied God in His abounding kindness and mercy. For of Him we read: " He loveth righteousness and justice " ; which means that the earth is filled with the lovingkindness of God.' To follow such a course is not an easy task, and can only be achieved by great efforts. Will it be too difficult, however, for him that has the fear of God always before him to gain this quality ? No; it will easily be gained by him whose every act is done in the love and fear of the Lord.

## FAITH IN GOD REWARDED

Rabbi Eliezer, Rabbi Joshua, and Rabbi Akiba, travelled about each year to collect money for the poor. Amongst the many charitable people who helped them with money, none gave more cheerfully and liberally than a man called Aben-Judan, who was a very rich man. Fortune, however, turned against this good man, as a dreadful storm destroyed the produce of his lands; a raging plague swept away the greater part of his flocks and herds; and his large fields and vineyards were immediately seized by those to whom money was due. Of all his vast possessions nothing was left to him but one small piece of land. Such a sudden misfortune was surely enough to depress any person. But Aben-Judan had been taught from his early youth to put his whole faith and trust in God, and to firmly believe that whatever He does is done for a good purpose, as He is a kind and Merciful Father, and is continually seeking to guard us from all unnecessary harm. He therefore accepted his fate with resignation and said: 'The Lord gave, and the Lord has taken away; may His name be praised for ever and ever.' He then patiently commenced to cultivate the piece of land which had remained to him, and by hard work and strict economy he did his utmost to support himself and his family decently; and was, notwithstanding his poverty, cheerful and contented. The next year came and one day he noticed the three Rabbis coming at a distance. It was then that his former affluence and his present sad condition rushed to his mind; and he felt for the first time the pangs of poverty. 'What *was* Aben-Judan,' he exclaimed, 'and what *is he now*?' Feeling very sad and dejected, he seated himself in a corner of his hut. His wife noticed the sudden change. 'What ails thee?' she asked most tenderly. 'Art thou not well? Tell me, that I may prescribe for thy relief!' 'Would to God it were in thy power, but the Almighty Merciful God alone can heal the wounds which He inflicts,' replied the distressed man. 'Dost thou not remember the days when we were prosperous; when our corn fed the hungry; our fleeces clothed the naked, and our oil and wine refreshed the sad, troubled spirit of those who were afflicted. The orphans came round us and blessed us; and the widow's heart sang for joy. Then did we taste those heavenly pleasures which are the lot of the good and charitable. But now, alas! we cannot relieve the fatherless, nor him who wants help, we are ourselves poor and wretched. Seest thou not yonder good men coming for the charitable collection? They will call here too, but what have we to give them?' 'Do not be so sad, my dear husband,' replied his wife, 'we have still one field left; suppose we sell half of it and give the money for the use of the poor? We can then trust in God to help us to support ourselves from the remaining half of the field.'

A ray of joy lit up the good man's face. He followed his wife's advice, sold half the field, and when the Rabbis came, he gave them the money. The Rabbis accepted the money and entered his name on their list of contributors, and as they were leaving, they said to him: 'May the Lord restore thee to thy former position and prosperity!'

Aben-Judan now continued his work, and again felt

contented. He went to plough the small piece of land which he had left, and as he was going along the foot of the ox that drew the plough-share sank into the ground, and the beast was maimed. Aben-Judan immediately rushed to release the poor animal from its painful position, and as he did so he noticed something glittering in the hollow which the foot of the animal had made. He wondered what the glittering thing could be, and after digging the hole deeper he found, to his astonishment and great joy, that an immense treasure had been concealed in that spot. He took the treasure home, and from the money he obtained for it he was able to remove from the wretched hut in which he lived into a very nice house. He next repurchased the lands and possessions which had been left to him by his forefathers, and which his distress had forced him to sell. He remembered the poor, and again became a father to the fatherless and a blessing to the unfortunate. The time again arrived when the three Rabbis came to make their usual collection for the poor. Not finding Aben-Judan in the place where he had lived the year before, they enquired of some people what had become of him, and how he was. 'Aben-Judan!' they exclaimed, 'the good and generous! Who is like him in riches, charity and goodness? See you yonder flocks and herds, those vast fields, flourishing vineyards and beautiful gardens? They are all belonging to Aben-Judan."

Whilst they were talking the good man happened to pass by, and he was greeted by the Rabbis. 'Rabbis,' he said, 'your blessing has produced plenty of fruit, so come to my house and partake of it. I will also make up the amount which I was unable to give you last year.' They followed him to his house, where, after entertaining them, he gave them a very handsome present for the poor. They accepted it and, taking out the subscription list of the previous year, said to him: 'See! Although many people gave larger contributions than you, yet we have placed your name at the top of the list; we knew that your sacrifice was greater than theirs, and that the smallness of the amount was from want of means. It is to men like you that the wise King Solomon referred when he said: "A man's gift extendeth his possessions, and leadeth him before the great"' (Proverbs, xviii, 1).

## CHARITY

KINDLY acts are far greater than almsgiving. Alms one can only give with money or money's worth, and only to the living and the poor; but kindliness can be bestowed without money, on the rich as well as on the poor, and even on the dead.

A Rabbi was once strolling along the sea beach and saw an almost naked man, who had just been saved from a shipwreck. The Rabbi approached the man, took him home, fed and clothed him, gave him money to enable him to continue his journey, and accompanied him a part of the way. Some time afterwards a neighbouring nation attacked some of the cities of Palestine and seized many Jews in order to sell them as slaves. The same Rabbi was chosen as the messenger to go to the king of the nation who had attacked the cities, and ask for the release of the captured Jews, for which he was to give five hundred pieces of silver as a ransom. When the Rabbi came before the king, he was greatly surprised to find that the king's chief minister was no other than the man whom he had helped with food, clothes and money. The minister at once recognised him and, upon hearing the purpose of the Rabbi's visit, pleaded for him to the king; the Jews were released, and the five hundred pieces of silver were given to the Rabbi as a present. The Rabbi then quoted the words of Solomon: 'Cast thy bread upon the waters, for thou shalt find it after many days' (Ecclesiastes, xi, 1).

Despise not the poor, thou knowest not how soon it may be thine own fate to be poor.

A General, named Turnus Rufus, once put the following question to Rabbi Akiba: 'If it is true, as I have very often heard you say, that your God is a friend of the poor, then why does He not support them, but permits them to continue to live in poverty?' 'The reason', answered the Rabbi, 'is that we may have the merit of relieving them, and thereby be saved from the tortures of eternal punishment.' 'And why do you call this a good deed?' asked the General. 'I should rather call it a bad deed, and deserving of the tortures of eternal punishment. Supposing a King was angry with one of his slaves, and ordered him to be imprisoned and suffer hunger and thirst, would not the King have just reason to be displeased with anyone who dared to provide the slave with either food or drink ? ' ' Suppose instead ', said the Rabbi, ' that the King's anger fell upon one of his own sons, and that, in a moment of anger, he forbade his son either food or drink, would he not be grateful to anyone who relieved the distress of his son ? Besides, it is the will of God that we should relieve the distress of the poor; for He has so declared by the prophet Isaiah, "O break thy bread to the hungry, and bring the distressed poor into thy house "' (Isaiah, lviii, 7).

Poverty is no proof of the disfavour of God, and we must not neglect our duty to the poor by finding excuses. If the poor can still call God their Father, it must be our duty to treat them as brethren.

He who hesitates in performing the duty of charity becomes guilty of committing a sin. This is proved in the life of Rabbi Nachum, who was surnamed Gamzu, because whatever happened to him he was in the habit of saying ' Gamzu Letovah ', which means 'This is also for some good purpose'. This Rabbi was blind, he was unable to use his hands, his feet were so sore that he had to keep them in water, and they were later amputated, and his body was covered with sores. His disciples once asked him: ' Since you are such a righteous man, why are you so sorely afflicted ? ' ' All my afflictions were brought upon me by myself,' answered the Rabbi. ' I once went to pay a visit to my father-in-law, and I took with me, as a present, three asses; one laden with various sorts of eatables, one laden with wine, and the third laden with various sorts of sweetmeats. When I was not far from the end of my journey a poor unhappy man, who was on the brink of starvation, called to me: " Master," he cried, " O! relieve my distress." " Wait ", I answered, " until I have unloaded the asses." This took up some time, and scarcely had I finished unloading the animals when the poor man dropped down dead before me. My conscience began to reprove me most severely. " Poor lamented man," I said, " a little more promptness might have saved thee, whilst my lack of thought has caused the delay which has killed thee." I then threw myself on his dead body and exclaimed: " O ! you eyes, that could but did not look at the distress of this poor man, may you also be deprived of the light of day; your hands, that would not reach him timely relief, may you also have no more use; you legs, that did not quickly run to his assistance, may you also no more be able to perform your usual duty; may this body, too, which did not feel sufficient pity for the misery and sadness of this lifeless body, also feel the affliction which you would not relieve." All that I said happened. This, then, is the cause of my misery.' The disciples, who were moved by this sad recital, but still more by their master's dreadful sufferings, exclaimed: ' Woe be to us, to see you in so pitiful a condition!' 'It would be very much worse for me', replied the heroic Rabbi, 'were you not to see me in this condition.' Meaning that he willingly endured his present sufferings as an atonement for his previous sins, in the hope of enjoying, in the next world, that happiness which is reserved for the good and the righteous.

Rabbi Akiba once said to Rabbi Tarphon, who was a very wealthy man but was not as charitable as he should have been according to his means: 'Shall I invest some money for you in an investment which will be very profitable to you?' Rabbi Tarphon agreed, and gave Rabbi Akiba four hundred *denars* of gold to be invested by him, which Akiba merely divided amongst the poor. After some time had passed, Rabbi Tarphon and Rabbi Akiba met, and the investment was discussed. Rabbi Akiba led his friend to a college, and asked a little boy to recite something from the Psalms. The boy recited: 'He hath scattered, he hath given to the needy; His righteousness endureth for ever' (Psalm cxii, 9). 'Thy property is with David, the King of Israel,' said Rabbi Akiba. 'Why hast thou done this?' said Rabbi Tarphon. 'Could I not have distributed the money myself to the poor, without your help?' 'No,' answered Akiba, 'it is a greater virtue to cause another person to give charity than to give oneself.'

A Rabbi was once told of a poor person who had been wealthy but had suffered much misfortune, and he therefore went to the man and said: 'I believe you will soon be receiving some money. I will meanwhile be glad to lend you some money for your business, and then you can pay me back when you are no longer in need.' The offer having been made in this way, the poor man gladly accepted the money, and was then given to understand that it was not a loan, but a gift.

Charity and kindly acts are Israel's pleaders before the Throne of Mercy.

During the reign of a certain King there was a very severe famine, and although the people had sold all their possessions they were still in the greatest distress. The King commanded that all his treasures should be sold, and the money be spent on corn and other necessities which should be distributed amongst those who were in need. The King's brothers, who were very grieved to see such a large amount of money being sacrificed, argued with the King and sought to cause him to change his mind from his intended generosity. 'Your fathers', they said, 'took care to add to the treasures which had been left to them by their fathers; but you not only neglect to add to those treasures which were left to you, but you even waste that which was left by them.' 'You are very much mistaken, my brethren,' answered the King. 'I, too, am providing treasures as they have done before me; but they provided earthly treasures, whilst I am providing heavenly treasures. They put them where earthly hands could reach them and they bore no fruit; whilst my treasures are unapproachable and are bearing very much fruit. They enjoyed their treasures in this world, whilst my treasures will be enjoyed in the world to come. They saved wealth whilst I am saving lives.'

Always remember the great value of charity, and the heavenly value of good deeds.

# INDEX